Eve's Orphans

Contributions in Women's Studies

Women's Studies: An Interdisciplinary Collection
Kathleen O'Connor Blumhagen and Walter D. Johnson, editors

Latin American Women: Historical Perspectives
Asunción Lavrin

Beyond Her Sphere: Women and the Professions in American
History
Barbara J. Harris

Literary America, 1903–1934: The Mary Austin Letters
T. M. Pearce, editor

The American Woman in Transition: The Urban Influence,
1870–1920
Margaret Gibbons Wilson

Liberators of the Female Mind: The Shirreff Sisters, Educational
Reform, and the Women's Movement
Edward W. Ellsworth

The Jewish Feminist Movement in Germany: The Campaigns of the
Jüdischer Frauenbund, 1904–1938
Marion A. Kaplan

Silent Hattie Speaks: The Personal Journal of Senator
Hattie Caraway
Diane D. Kincaid, editor

Women in Irish Society: The Historical Dimension
Margaret MacCurtain and Donncha O'Corrain

Margaret Fuller's *Woman in the Nineteenth Century:*
A Literary Study of Form and Content, of Sources and Influence
Marie Mitchell Olesen Urbanski

To Work and to Wed: Female Employment, Feminism, and the Great
Depression
Lois Scharf

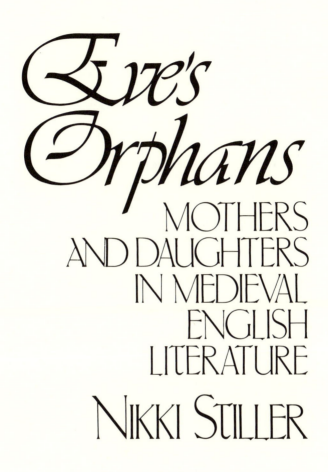

Eve's Orphans

MOTHERS AND DAUGHTERS IN MEDIEVAL ENGLISH LITERATURE

NIKKI STILLER

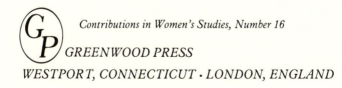

Contributions in Women's Studies, Number 16

GREENWOOD PRESS

WESTPORT, CONNECTICUT · LONDON, ENGLAND

Library of Congress Cataloging in Publication Data
Stiller, Nikki
  Eve's orphans

  (Contributions in women's studies ; no. 16
ISSN 0147-104X)
  Bibliography: p.
  Includes index.
  1. English literature—Middle English, 1100—1500
History and criticism. 2. Mothers and daughters in
literature. 3. Women in literature. I. Title.
II. Series.
PR275.M64S77   820'.9'001   79-8954
ISBN 0-313-22067-0 lib. bdg.

Library of Congress Catalog Card Number: 79-8954
ISBN: 0-313-22067-0
ISSN: 0147-104X

First published in 1980

Greenwood Press
A division of Congressional Information Service, Inc.
88 Post Road West, Westport, Connecticut 06881
Printed in the United States of America
10 9 8 7 6 5 4 3 2 1

ACKNOWLEDGMENTS

Grateful acknowledgment is made to the following publishers:

Oxford University Press for permission to reprint extracts from *The Works of Geoffrey Chaucer*, edited by F. N. Robinson, 2d ed. © F. N. Robinson 1957; *Early Middle English Verse and Prose*, edited by J. A. W. Bennett and G. V. Smithers. © Oxford University Press 1966; *Sir Gawain and the Green Knight*, edited by J. R. R. Tolkien and E. V. Gordon, 2d. ed. revised by Norman Davies. © Oxford University Press 1967; *Floris and Blanchefleur*, edited by A. B. Taylor, 1927. By permission of Oxford University Press.

J M Dent & Sons Ltd and E. P. Dutton for permission to reprint extracts from *Arthurian Romances* by Chrétien de Troyes, trans. W. W. Comfort, 1914 and *Lays of Marie De France and Other French Legends*, trans. by Eugene Mason, 1954, Everyman's Library Series.

Maurice Valency for permission to reprint extracts from *In Praise of Love* (New York: Farrar, Straus & Giroux, 1975).

The Huntington Library and Art Gallery for permission to reprint extracts from *The Middle English Miracles of the Virgin* by Beverley Boyd, 1964. Reprinted with the permission of the Henry E. Huntington Library and Art Gallery.

University of Kansas Press for permission to reprint extracts from *From Camelot to Joyous Garde*, trans. J. Neale Cameron, 1974.

Chatto and Windus Ltd. for permission to reprint extracts from *Courtiers' Trifles* by Walter Map, edited and translated by Frederich Tupper and Marbury Bladen Ogle, 1924.

Houghton Mifflin Company for permission to reprint extracts from *The Works of Geoffrey Chaucer*, 2d ed., edited by F. N. Robinson. Copyright © 1957 by F. N. Robinson. Reprinted by permission of Houghton Mifflin Company.

Penguin Books Ltd. for permission to reprint extracts from Sir Thomas Malory, *Le Morte D'Arthur*, edited by Janet Cowen (The Penguin English Library, 1969), vols. 1 and 2.

Librairie Honore Champion for permission to reprint extracts from *Tristan and Iseult* by Beroul, trans. Janet Hille-Caulkins and Guy R. Mermier, 1967.

Nelson-Hall for permission to reprint extracts from *The Knightly Tales of Sir Gawain*, edited by Lewis B. Hall, 1976.

Early English Text Society for permission to reprint extracts from O.S. Osbern Bokenham *Legendys of Hooly Wommen*, edited by Mary S. Serjeantson, 1960.

Search Press for permission to reprint extracts from *The Revelations of Divine Love* by Julian of Norwich, edited by Dom. Roger Hudleston, O.S.B. Copyright © Burns and Oates, 1952.

For Blanche Stiller, my mother,
who gave me the gifts of her struggle

CONTENTS

Acknowledgments   *v*
Preface   *xi*

1 The Great Unwritten Story   3
2 Life with Father: The Iron Dowry   15
3 Natural Mothers: The Powerless Mirror   39
4 The Fantasy of Power: Old Hags and
    Ancient Crones   63
5 Fostermothers: Women Mothering Women   93
6 Eve's Orphans   127

Bibliographical Notes   *145*
Index   *149*

PREFACE

Only a decade or so ago it was rather bad form for a woman to mention her mother favorably in public. Alienation and hostility were held to be the hallmarks of adulthood among many who considered themselves psychologically, emotionally, and sexually liberated. Whether the American second- and third-generation drive for social ascendancy exacerbated the misogynistic tendency to disavow the female parent I do not know, but it seems that a dozen years went by before women began to realize that it was in the interests of a still patriarchal society to teach women of different generations to dislike and even to hate each other: to teach mothers, for example, to resent their daughters' youth, and to teach daughters to scorn the women who had brought them into the world and who in certain cases, to be sure, had helped to bind their minds as effectively as Chinese women had once helped bind their daughters' feet.

But some of us had had different experiences, and trusting to these experiences rather than to what the medieval English would have referred to as "auctorité"—accepted authority—we began to perceive some mothers as the victims instead of the villains of history, and some as heroic in their struggle to maintain their integrity as human beings and in their whole-hearted devotion to their female children. That is the real meaning of the women's movement: the restoration of creative selfhood to all human beings and a new respect for kindness, generosity, and love.

Academe has also witnessed changes of late. Histories of the family, of manners, of childhood begin to appear—or are reissued after having long been ignored. The women's movement has opened new paths for the literary scholar and critic and has raised new questions about our judgments and, ultimately, our values. How has predominantly male authorship, for instance, influenced the content and style of what we read and what we approve in our reading? Does a man write differently for a female audience than for a male one? Do women authors choose to write on different subjects than men do, or do they treat the same subjects in a different way? Has our world—including our psyches—been distorted in this glass, or have the great poets overcome the historical obstacles of sexual segregation and misogyny?

I have chosen to explore medieval English literature in regard to these feminist and philosophical issues not only because it is the field I know best but also because I believe we are the inheritors, for better or for worse, of that culture, which itself contains elements of the Celtic, the Graeco-Latin, the Judaic, and the Provençal. Few otherwise well-read people have more than a cursory knowledge of medieval English literature, perhaps because of the necessary past dominance of philology in the field. Now, however, the words, phrases, and constructs are probably as clear as they ever will be, and I hope we will be fortunate enough to see medieval literary artifacts treated as such. Translations are necessary if one is to address readers who did not happen to specialize in Chaucer or in thirteenth-century English prose. In this volume, I have incorporated my own translations—unless otherwise noted—into the text and have included the original Middle English material in the notes.

An inquiry of the kind that follows could not have been undertaken twenty years ago. Even now, the paucity of material is astounding, but one finds that interest abounds. When women, from those in their first year in college to those well into their eighties, look for their history they want increasingly to know about the world through which their mothers and grandmothers and great-grandmothers moved, a world which—they are now aware—was substantially different from that of the men.

Naturally, I was moved by my own experiences to write this book. My mother, an immigrant and working woman, has given me unfailing support in my intellectual endeavors and provided an outstanding model for me in her respect for womankind. Other women have helped and encouraged me along the way: Mary deKay, Barbara Zung Kokot, Helaine Newstead of The City University of New York, and Lizzi Rosenberger of Tel-Aviv. Women, I have found, celebrate each other's accomplishments. It is telling that when my typist, Wanda Lewis, heard of this book's forthcoming publication, she called *her* mother to give her the good news.

Eve's Orphans

THE GREAT UNWRITTEN STORY

*"This cathexis between mother and daughter...
is the great unwritten story."*
—Adrienne Rich[1]

"The Clerk's Tale" is clearly an allegory. Chaucer's pious narrator intends to reveal, in the relation of wife to husband, the soul's relation to God. The clerk's extreme position must also be seen as the result of his rhetorical competition with the Wife of Bath and in the context of the wide range of positions made manifest in the tales of the marriage group. In reading *The Canterbury Tales*, however, although the Prioress' anti-Semitism, the Merchant's bitterness, and the Wife of Bath's lust for power yield to a careful explication and become assimilated, Griselda's loyalty to the man she thinks has had her children slain remains beyond imaginative acceptance.[2]

What kind of a mother is this? Such a question trespasses upon the territory of art, yet calls for an investigation. Griselda's meek obedience to Walter—over and above the corpses of her young ones, as it were—contradicts contemporary notions about the power of the mothering instinct, the latent strength one has come to believe even the most abject and exploited women have possessed. The untenable, almost unthinkable, nature of Griselda's obedience indicates a different set of priorities. Although these priorities are set forth in the misogynous and exaggerated version of the clerk, this discrepancy appears so basic as to be shocking, even if one allows for satiric and allegorical ends. A woman's devotion to the well-being of her children appears, from "The Clerk's Tale," not to have been an absolute cultural value. At this point, it is not difficult to go a bit further to perceive that perhaps our concept of motherhood and the medieval concept of motherhood are not quite the same.

Adelaide Evans Harris, in her book on *The Heroine of the Middle English Romances*, remarks that mothers, in these romances, are conspicuously absent.[3] At first this seems to be true not only of the romances but of all the major works in poetry and prose of England and of France in the period between the Norman Conquest and the early sixteenth century.[4] If a few mothers do come to mind, they appear in conjunction with their sons, or in relation to other men. Chrétien's Percival has a mother and is gently mocked for being something of a mama's boy, in fact, until he learns better from his tutelary knights.[5] Mothers and sons appear in Scots ballads,[6] and the Virgin Mother emerges as very clearly compassionate towards men in, for example, the German legends of the late Middle Ages.[7] But even the connection of male children with their mothers comes as a surprise to the reader; in the literary mainstream of the medieval period, a character with an influential mother is a rarity, no matter what the gender of that character. Although the male authorship of most works has a great deal to do with the phenomenon, the persistant denigration or total obliteration of the mother's role found in medieval works testifies to a misogyny so deep and fearful that it is difficult for an individual living in the twentieth century to comprehend it.

I do not intend to take on the problem of misogyny as such in the medieval period; my concern here will be with mothers and daughters and their interrelationship and with those who are portrayed in mother-daughter roles. Nevertheless, certain matters touching on the hatred of women call for clarification, as the general attitude of the male population —or that part of it which was articulate—has some bearing on the subject at hand. Nowhere is this attitude more evident, in former centuries as in our own, than in writing on creation and on childbirth; for where else is the biological difference between men and women more clearly manifested? In what other capacity can woman claim a power so clearly her own?

Christianity did little to temper the misogyny of the ancient world, but the Church was not the sole source of bitter hatred.[8] Womb envy has long been repressed by the Western consciousness, and such repression testifies to its power, as both Bruno Bettelheim and Phyllis Chesler have shown.[9] Some have seen the denigration of women and the denial of their sexual or biological capacities as symptomatic of such a repression.[10] In the *Timaeus*, for example, in which Plato sets forth his creation myth, the philosopher considers the Demiurgos, the cosmological equivalent of the male, to be the dominant principle and the cause of creation; the womb, the cosmic "nurse" or "receptacle," as it is called, is seen as secondary and passive and whatever takes place there as unfathomed, unknown.[11] Aristotle, seeing a woman as an incomplete male,[12] nonetheless in his embryology presents a view that constitutes an *advancement* as he allows that the female might contribute "material for the semen to work upon."[13] The older Graeco-Egyptian doctrine, which exerted tremendous influence, according to Joseph Needham,[14] denied that the mother was a parent of the child at all and stipulated that she simply provided a *nidus* in which the male seed developed.[15] This view is set forth in the Middle Ages in such highly respected and well-known works as the *De Formatione Corporis* of Giles of Rome and the *Sentences* commentary by Richard of Middleton.[16] While Thomas Aquinas adopts a modified version of the Aristotelian doctrine, he still gives the mother secondary powers of generation:

> the generative power of the female is imperfect compared to that of the male; for just as in the crafts, the inferior workman prepares the material and the more skilled operator shapes it, so likewise the female generative virtue provides the substance but the active male virtue makes it into the finished product.[17]

The doctrine of male generation or creativity certainly reinforced the view of woman as an inferior creature, even if it did arise from man's envy of the female's capacity to bear children.[18] Whatever the psychological roots of the theory, becoming pregnant and becoming a mother did not arouse respect or insure power. As Ann S. Haskell points out, "the single most important requirement for the conduct of a medieval woman of any social stratum was subordination."[19] Women could exercise authority over their children as little as over other parts of their lives; this was true for queens as well as for commoners, and perhaps more so at times, as the common law seems to have granted women authority through custom now and again.[20] Among women of the nobility, it is fairly clear that mothers and their children were alienated beings, alienated even in the physical sense: babies were given over to wet nurses shortly after birth, children were sent to neighboring courts to learn noble ways, and marriages were contracted, if not always consummated, at tender ages.[21] Thus it is not true, as Maurice Valency claims in an otherwise excellent work, that mother-child bonds have remained stable throughout the development of Western culture.[22] The sharp separation of mother and child usual in the upper classes might have served, it has been suggested,[23] to prevent traumatic emotional involvement in a period when infant mortality rates were extremely high. It seems to me, however, that the estrangement of mother and child may well have contributed to a loosening, if not a severance, of the mother-child bond, a provision, albeit unconscious, by the patriarchy against the formation of a very strong loyalty between child and mother.

If mothers are conspicuously absent in medieval literature, the same cannot be said of fathers. The sway of the *paterfamilias* in European history is no longer in dispute.[24] If fathers fought to control their sons and legislated to possess their wives as chattels, their control over their daughters seems to have been as close to absolute as possible without actual enslavement.[25] From ancient times well into the Renaissance, daughters passed from their fathers' hands into those of their husbands or other male guardians; whether for dowries or for gifts to abbeys enabling the women to become nuns, daughters were dependent upon their fathers' good will.[26] Power, of course, creates its own relationships, and these we see portrayed in romances, popular poems, and the lives of female saints.[27]

"A woman," Anne Sexton wrote, "*is* her mother / That's the main thing."[28] But even if women were dependent upon their fathers economically, socially, and, to a great extent, psychologically; even if men scorned motherhood; and even if women were distanced from their children of either sex, relationships between mothers and children, and between mothers and daughters in particular, must have existed. In what other way could generation after generation of girls have learned how to be women? For the role of mother, and the role of daughter who is to become in turn a mother herself, could have been learned only in part from men.[29]

In a book about eunuchs, *The Keeper of the Bed*, Charles Humana justifies his use of storytellers' testimony from the *Arabian Nights* by noting that the storytellers received "first-hand impressions" contemporary scholars had not.[30] As official history has paid even less attention to mothers and daughters than to eunuchs, the same justification seems appropriate for exploring the mother-daughter relationship through literature. This path to the past has its hazards, however. Art is not life and life is not art, although the "truths" of history or of historians and/or chroniclers in the medieval period seem as dubious in objectivity as the records of poets.

More narrowly, two major methodological problems are presented by considerations of social class and male authorship. As only the clergy and the gentlefolk were literate—and poets dealt primarily with members of their own caste—little extant poetry or prose depicts life in the third estate. Thus, much of what can be culled from medieval literature about mothers and daughters will be about aristocratic mothers and daughters. The great difficulty presented by the predominantly male authorship of medieval works, I believe, is not so much misogyny as a distortion through ignorance. There existed in medieval society as in the classical world, a kind of sexual segregation, as Sarah Pomeroy makes clear in *Women in Antiquity.* In Chrétien's France as in Pomeroy's Greece, many important parts of women's lives were hidden from men's eyes. Given even the largest heart and most humane mind—given the powers of observation of Chaucer, for example—what went on beside the child-bed or while the ladies were dressing or between two gossips—Chaucer does not recount *that* conversation in "The Wife of Bath's Tale"—was difficult of access. There are exceptions. The authors of the *Ancrene Riwle* and *Hali Meidenhad* seem to have known and liked women and to have been acquainted with their private ways.[31] Popular literature, primarily drama, yields some depictions of women in their own world; and in the major authors, now and then a scene in which women converse may be found. But on the whole the world in which women moved —that of the spinning room and the bedchamber—lay outside the province of men's knowledge. Thus, even when women take active roles in medieval literature, these roles are primarily romantic and male-centered. This holds true for much Marian imagery as well as for that of courtly love.[32]

Given these limitations and difficulties, however, if we look hard enough and close enough, through all the barriers of class, male authorship, and paternal domination, we begin to glimpse our mothers at last in an occasional reference, a fleeting portrait, or in a whole series of substitutes and surrogates: a hidden gallery in a closed-off wing. Powerful historical figures demand our attention: the courtly ladies of southern France; Christine de Pisan; Eloise and Saint Theresa; the Paston letter-writers; the women for whom the minnesingers sang; Marie de France and Marie de Champagne; and a little later, Anne Boleyn and Katherine Parr. These are only a few. In the literature, also, various women stand out: Iseult or Isolde, Guenevere, Morgan le Fay; the Wife of Bath, Dorigen, the Prioress; and the Duchess Blanche and, of course, Criseyde. In fictionalized accounts we find St. Margaret, St. Katherine, and the Empress Helene, as well as those like Julian of Norwich and Margery Kempe who come to us in created voices of their own making. How did these women become what they were? How, in reference to the male-authored female characters, did men see them becoming what they were?

A number of these women seem to have been male-identified, especially the female saints. Although some of the saints are descended from another tradition and another literature, the more egalitarian Anglo-Saxon, and retain certain qualities derived from that culture, the increased strength of the patriarchy in the medieval period proper manifests itself in the strivings of these women, historical and fictitious, to act like, feel like, and be like men.[33] Their characteristic virginity illustrates an important dilemma and paradox: in order to be virtuous and yet potent in one's own right, according to the Church Fathers and the medieval schoolmen, a woman had to become like a man, yet in doing so she had to deny both biological truth and natural sexual affiliation. Vern L. Bullough, in an invaluable article on "Medieval Medical Views of Women," summarizes the opinion of Philo on this subject: "progress," for the influential Philo, means giving up the female gender, that is, the passive corporeal and sense perception, for the male gender, representing the active incorporeal and rational thought; "the easiest way for a woman to approach the male level of rationality was by remaining a virgin."[34] The powerful virgin, the Artemis figure, the chaste sister, is permitted to control her own life to a certain extent but in exchange must repudiate the demands and gifts of her own body, must scorn the memory of having been born of a woman, and must reject her own ability to bear children. The virgin, that is, does not really reject sexuality as such, and in the abstract, for sexuality appears in much religious writing in a sublimated form, in the motifs, for example, of the nun as the bride of Christ and in the elaborate use of the Song of Songs. What the woman pledged to virginity had to reject was motherhood and true daughterhood. She had to forfeit being like her mother in the most essential way. Indeed, many of these female figures seem to be the children of men alone, and not their mothers' daughters.

Mothering a daughter means not only to sustain and nurture, obviously the first mothering function in regard to both sexes, but also to be a model and guide to another creature like oneself.[35] Individuals form identifications not simply on the basis of gender, of course, but in regard to various personality traits: a daughter, for example, may identify with her father's neatness and her mother's agility. Ideally, identifications would not be circumscribed by gender; within the tradition that stretches from the ancient world to our own times, however, identifications that cross gender lines have been extremely problematic.[36] Physical prowess, for instance, considered a male or "masculine" characteristic within the culture, tends to endanger the sexual identity of a woman who has identified with a parent's physical prowess; such a woman might find her identity as a woman questioned and even threatened. Certain kinds of identifications, then, have not been transsexual: men have in general learned the characteristic signs of "masculinity" from men, and women the characteristic traits of "femininity" from women, with no end of psychological complications, to be sure, and probably with great human impoverishment.

However, an aversion to the premises and effects of a given system should not blind us to the historical necessity involved, nor interfere with our seeing how—crudely and perhaps wastefully and mistakenly—a system lasted because it provided a means of survival. Identification by gender has been the dominant course of transmission for character traits and modes of behavior, and women have survived. One of the purposes of this book is to discover just how medieval women might have taught their daughters to survive in a world ruled entirely by men, to find what models of conduct mothers gave their daughters so that the daughters could, in turn, reproduce their own kind in more than a biological sense.

Most striking in the literature of the medieval period, in relation to questions raised here, is the amount of mothering performed by women other than natural mothers. Natural mothers do relate to their daughters in the literature, and the overall attitude is one of sympathy and passive support. Because of the powerlessness of the mother and her estrangement from the child, however, the support is very passive indeed.[37] Women learned to be women in large part through identification with women other than their mothers, with mother surrogates and foster mothers. Women are represented in medieval literature as mothering each other. The bonds between these women, although they are drawn none too frequently and none too explicitly in a literature composed by men, seem to have been strong; the protecting, sheltering impulse and the desire to keep the other woman from hurt seem to have prevailed.

Even Griselda, that misery of a natural mother who is willing to sacrifice her own children to her husband's whim and her vow to obey, overcomes her humility and speaks out when she is asked to prepare the wedding feast for her husband's new wife:

> "One thing I beg of you, and also warn:
> That you do not prick with torments
> This tender maiden, as you did to me;
> For she was brought up in her girlhood
> More tenderly, and, so I think,
> She could not endure adversity
> As could a creature brought up in poverty."[38]

Griselda does not know at this point that the lovely young girl is really her natural daughter whom Walter has not in fact had slain. Her impulse is to shield this woman as much as she can from the harshness of the man and his demands.

Women have been and still are in many respects a nation of orphans. But even though Mother Eve for many centuries has been deprived of her daughters, women have provided models for other women, have sustained bonds one can only call familial, and have desired more frequently than is commonly thought to nurture, love, and protect each other in a hostile world. If we are recognizing the significance of this behavior only now, we should not make the mistake of thinking it did not exist before, in our obscure and cloistered past. I would like to illuminate in these pages the tenacity and strength of the mother-daughter bond, natural or surrogate, through an investigation of English literature, with some excursions into that of related cultures, in the medieval period.

NOTES

1. Adrienne Rich, *Of Woman Born* (New York: W.W. Norton, 1976), p. 225.

2. I refer to *The Canterbury Tales* as edited by F. N. Robinson in *The Works of Geoffrey Chaucer* (Boston: Houghton-Mifflin, 1957).

3. (Cleveland: Western Reserve University Press, 1928), p. 38.

4. I take the liberty of extending the medieval period beyond its traditional closure at 1400 because attitudes towards women tend to change slowly.

5. Chrétien de Troyes, *Perceval le Gallois,* trans. Lucien Foulet (Paris: Agnizet, 1970).

6. *See* "Lord Randall" or the oedipal "Edward," in which the mother has urged the son to kill his father.

7. *See* Johannes Herolt, *Miracles of the Blessed Virgin Mary,* trans. C. C. Swinton Bland (London: Routledge, 1928), and Beverly Boyd, ed., *The Middle English Miracles of the Virgin* (San Marion, Cal.: The Huntington Library, 1964).

8. Vern L. Bullough, "Medieval Medical and Scientific Views of Women," *Viator* 4 (1973): 485–501.

9. Bruno Bettelheim, *Symbolic Wounds* (New York: Collier Books, 1971), and Phyllis Chesler, *About Men* (New York: Simon and Schuster, 1978).

10. R. E. L. Masters, *Eros and Evil* (Baltimore: Penguin, 1974), pp. 170–2.

11. *See* Frederick Copleston, S.J., "Physics of Plato," in *A History of Philosophy,* vol. 1 (Westminster, Maryland: The Newman Press, 1963), pp. 244–52.

12. *See* Bullough, "Views of Women," pp. 485–7.

13. Aristotle, *De Generatione Animalium,* trans. A. L. Peck (London: Loeb Classics, 1943), p. 275.

14. Joseph Needham, *A History of Embryology* (New York: Abelard-Schuman, 1959), pp. 43–4.

15. Ibid., p. 43.

16. *See* M. Anthony Hewson, *Giles of Rome and the Medieval Theory of Conception* (London: Atholone Press, 1975), pp. 46–7, and p. 69 in particular.

17. Cited by Needham, *Embryology,* p. 93; *Summa Theologica,* pt. 1, qu. lxxvi, art. 3.

18. This is Chesler's contention; *see* note 9.

19. Ann S. Haskell, "The Paston Women on Marriage in Fifteenth Century England," *Viator* 4 (1973): 459–71; this on p. 459.

20. *See* Sylvia Thrupp, *The Merchant Class of Medieval London* (Chicago: University of Chicago Press, 1948), pp. 170–3.

21. Haskell, "The Paston Women," p. 469; Harris, *The Heroine,* pp. 38ff.

22. Maurice Valency, *In Praise of Love* (New York: Farrar, Straus and Giroux, 1975), pp. 14–5.

23. Haskell, "The Paston Women."

24. On the rise of patriarchal power in the ancient world, *see* Sarah Pomeroy, *Goddesses, Whores, Wives and Slaves: Women in Antiquity* (New York: Schocken, 1975); on the socioemotional implications of patriarchy, *see* Mary Daly, *Beyond God the Father* (Boston: Beacon Press, 1973).

25. *See* Haskell, "The Paston Women," on forced marriage; *see also* Roberta Frank, "Marriage in Twelfth and Fifteenth Century Iceland," *Viator* 4 (1973): 473ff.

26. Doris Mary Stenton, *English Society in the Early Middle Ages* (London: Penguin, 1951), pp. 73–5.

27. *See* Daly, *Beyond God the Father*.

28. In the frequently anthologized poem "Houses."

29. One of the more interesting and explicit documents pertaining to this is the exchange between mothers and daughters in *The Paston Letters* where the mothers attempt to teach the daughters, often very cruelly, to submit. Haskell, "The Paston Women," p. 470, thinks the mothers did so in order to permit the daughters, later, to command; whether or not this is so, the attempt to form the daughter is illuminating. *See* James Gairdner, ed., *The Paston Letters* (New York: AMS Press, 1965), nos. 185 and 196.

30. Charles Humana, *The Keeper of the Bed: the Story of the Eunuch* (London: Arlington Books, 1973), pp. 8–9.

31. These two works in early Middle English, discussed at length in Chapter 3, are directed at female audiences; the first, in fact was composed at the behest of female religious leaders.

32. Valency, *In Praise of Love*, p. 37: "The Provençal *chanson*, as we might expect in the poetry of a male society, directed itself to the female, but it focused interest unequivocally on the male."

33. The growing strength of the patriarchy can be seen in comparing Anglo-Saxon female saints' lives with post-Conquest redactions, i.e., that of St. Juliana. *See* chapter 2.

34. Bullough, "Views of Women," p. 497.

35. Psychology recognizes differences in the entire process of identification; *see* Sigmund Freud, "Female Sexuality," *Collected Papers*, vol. 5 (London: Hogarth Press, 1956), pp. 252–72.

36. *See* Karen Horney, *Feminine Psychology*, ed. Harold Kelman (New York: W.W. Norton, 1967).

37. Haskell ("The Paston Women," pp. 468ff.) claims the attitude of medieval mothers in regard to their daughters wa "intractable," but H. S. Bennett in *The Pastons and Their England* (London: Cambridge University Press, 1922), pp. 75–83, situates this attitude toward daughters within the general repressive and controlling behavior of the period.

38. Chaucer, *Works*, p. 112, 11. 1037–43:

> O thyng biseke I yow, and warne also,
> That ye ne prikke with no tormentynge
> This tendre mayden, as ye han doon mo;
> For she is fostred in hire norissynge
> More tendrely, and, to my supposynge,
> She koude nat adversitee endure
> As koude a povre fostred creature.

LIFE WITH FATHER: THE IRON DOWRY

🐾

"God's free daughter, and His Son's spouse. . . ."
—*Hali Meidenhad*[1]

In medieval times, all children were their father's children. For the most part, the embryology of the period supported the patriarchy's legal claim. Giles of Rome, one of the great schoolmen of the thirteenth century, held that "the male seed" is "a residue of the individual, meaning that it truly conveys human nature to the offspring. The female seed, on the other hand, cannot be regarded as a residue of the species or of the individual since it has no direct function in generation."[2] Furthermore, the notions of family and property having been intertwined from ancient times, the medieval father was not subject to pangs of remorse when he treated his wife and children as chattels.[3] The exercise of legal, moral, and religious control was seen not as a right but as a duty. Under German law, for example, which exerted considerable influence during the medieval period,

> German women spent their lives under constant tutelage, but the basis of their legal incapacity seems to have been rationalized not in terms of their moral or intellectual weakness but in terms of . . .their inability to maintain their rights by force of arms. German women were therefore, so to speak, in lifelong protective custody. A woman under the *mundium*, or right of wardship, could, in theory, do nothing without her guardian. He represented her at law and he controlled her property.[4]

As the *mundium* insured the passing of a daughter from her father's hands directly into those of husband or brother, the entire course of a woman's life might be determined by her relations with her father. It might be determined, that is, by her daughterhood, a status indicative of more dependence than that of wife, mother, or mistress because it combined the restrictions on women with the helplessness of childhood.

Power and control do not of course preclude affection. As we see in medieval English lilterature, although the institution of marriage was based on property and male power, Dorigen yearns for her husband as she looks out towards the treacherous rocks, and Sir Orfeo pines after Queen Heurodis.[5] Familial feelings can and do forge the irons of power. Such feelings maintain their hold on the individual through ambivalence. Authority and obedience, rage and fear, are compounded with love and the desire to please. Daughters, by dint of their sex and their dependent position within the family, were particularly vulnerable to the threats and blandishments of patriarchal authority.[6] Whatever the origins of that authority—whether springing from or contributing to the denigration of women—its complexity and influence in the medieval period call for an investigation of the father-daughter relationship to precede any exploration of the mother-daughter bond. It is almost impossible, that is, to comprehend the attitudes towards motherhood and daughterhood without clarifying the father's central position in a medieval woman's life and delineating the psychological effects of that role.

Parents appear omnipotent to the child because the child is incapable of providing for herself or himself. The child's very helplessness dictates an attempt to emulate the seemingly almighty parents in order to obtain some of their power.[7] Medieval daughters appear to have been as dependent upon their male parents as young children are today upon both parents. This dependency might well have been lifelong. Fathers determined the course of their daughters' lives, for example, in terms of simple economics, providing or not providing adult daughters with husbands and dowries, or sometimes giving them over to nunneries instead of men.[8] Young women needed their fathers for much more than childhood sustenance. They did not have recourse to armed rebellion if such provision was not forthcoming. The tendency to identify with the powerful father must have been strong, or perhaps one should say the predisposition to identify with him, because an overt masculine and active identification would have been considered disastrous for the female child or young woman, a putative wife and mother.[9] In reviewing the domestic education into which young women were forced, it becomes evident that great care was taken, perhaps unconsciously, to prevent any such natural identification from forming.[10]

The problem of masculine identification for daughters becomes clear in the lives of a number of women saints, such as Margaret, Christine, or Juliana. The most extreme yet in some ways paradigmatic of these is *þe Liflade ant te Passiun of Seinte Iuliene*.[11] It is doubtful that its author-redactor was aware of the ironies intrinsic to the plot, for in this tale of a woman fighting against father and suitor to preserve the integrity of her belief, both Juliana's emulation of masculine modes of behavior and the punishment she incurs through such emulation emerge.[12] Juliana's heroism stems from her resistance to male power, as much as anything else. The villains of the legend are pagans, yet it seems clear that if any young woman had demonstrated the same independence of thought and action in an entirely Christian milieu, the attitude of the men would have been similar to that of the unenlightened pagan torturers. Although the author obviously wishes to uphold patriarchal authority, Juliana's questioning of that authority and her rejection of the predefined feminine-passive role deliver a very different message to the contemporary reader.[13]

The basic plot of the life of St. Juliana, in its Latin, Anglo-Saxon, and Middle English versions, runs as follows: Juliana, the nubile daughter of a powerful pagan king, is promised in marriage by her father to one Eleusius, an up-and-coming young man in the service of the Roman Empire. She refuses to marry Eleusius, despite the alternating threats and promises of her father and her suitor, for different reasons in different versions, but primarily because she is a Christian. The father and the suitor beat and torture her or try with sweet words to make her yield. Even though her father is very powerful, Juliana cannot be made to submit to him, nor will she submit to the (male) powers of Rome, represented in the person of Eleusius. She also fights off a devil who visits her in the prison where father and suitor have cast her. The devil, an externalized part of her own nature, tries to tempt her, to lure her from her chosen path; but Juliana abides by the dictates of her conscience and continues to refuse to do the bidding of her father and her intended spouse. Finally, after being rescued several times by angels, the powers-that-be behead Juliana, and she becomes a martyr of the Church.

The older versions of the life of St. Juliana provide an opportunity to observe the similarities and the shifting emphases between the Latin/Anglo-Saxon variants and the considerably expanded Middle English texts. All the forms of the legend, C. W. Kennedy writes, "agree that a maiden named Juliana suffered martyrdom at the city of Nicodemia in the reign of Maximilian, Roman Emperor from 308–314."[14] Cynewulf used the basic legend "in the eighth century in the Anglo-Saxon poem called Juliana, which was based upon the Latin prose version included. . . in the Acta Sanctorum."[15] Thus, the legend passed through several cultures, taking on the characteristic coloration and preoccupation of each.

In the Latin version closest to the source, Juliana appears in a somewhat naturalistic milieu. Africanus, Juliana's father, is presented consistently in all versions as a fervent persecutor of Christians, but Juliana's mother, who influences the girl, is mentioned only in the Latin: the wife of Africanus, we learn, "in the intent of her heart abhorred the sacrilegious worship of Mars."[16] Juliana's beliefs, in the oldest version, do not arise *ex nihilo*, as it were, but from an atmosphere of religious doubt and struggle where women were perhaps more open to the new teachings.[17] Moreover, clear in this version but confused in later ones is the religious motivation for Juliana's rejection of Eleusius. Here she objects to him because he is a pagan, not because she wishes to forego the married state as such. She tells her suitor's messengers to report that she will marry him if he will worship "the Father and Son and Holy Ghost."[18] Although her virginity is mentioned and its power acknowledged in the prison scene where she struggles with her own particular demon, the author does not dwell upon its importance. Finally, Eleusius, Juliana's suitor, is the principal tormentor, whereas in the Middle English version her father shares equally in her torture.

In Cynewulf's Anglo-Saxon poem of the eighth century, Juliana resembles Deborah of the Old Testament as much as or more than a Middle English heroine. Although Anglo-Saxon poetry in general draws upon the spirit and text of the Hebrew heroic tradition,[19] the dignity accorded Juliana here might just as well have come from the Anglo-Saxon culture, in which women shared the work and seem to have been treated with respect.[20] The descriptions of women are for the most part measured and dignified, with obvious sympathy for the plight of widows and orphans in a society fraught with physical danger and constantly vulnerable to attack.[21] Wealhtheow in *Beowulf*, for example, not only serves the warriors graciously but gives them courage and rewards them for their bravery.[22] Cynewulf's presentation of a heroic woman has a wholeness and credibility that the other versions lack. Courage is not identified in this work as an exclusively male characteristic, and Cynewulf's Juliana sounds as if she speaks of her rights when she declares that Eleusius may not "by compulsion" take her to wife.[23] The Anglo-Saxon account also places no particular emphasis upon Juliana's virginity; the poet speaks of her as pure, but this may signify purity of spirit as well.[24]

While Cynewulf condemns the violence and brutality of Africanus and Eleusius, a violence inherent in their pagan ethic, he does not dwell upon that violence. Not so the Middle English redactor. The late twelfth-century or early thirteenth-century *Iuliene* contains as much gore as the Latin, perhaps more, described with a curious relish. The narrative point of view in this work is confused. Although the poem certainly describes the use and abuse of power, the narrator's explicit position, reverence for Juliana, is at variance with what emerges from the narration. Emerging from the displays of arbitrariness and cruelty is Juliana's own cruel vindictiveness; Juliana, throughout this work, shares the salient characteristic of the men in this work: aggression. For this quality she is called "unwomanliche," unwomanly.[25]

Juliana is not merely steadfast and forebearing; her behavior, albeit in the name of a Christian God, is a mirror image of that of Eleusius and her father. Moreover, she initiates the offensive by challenging her "fleshliche feeder" (her earthly father), her suitor, and the power of Rome; she tells them that they may do what they will to her in their anger, but she will no longer hide her beliefs.[26] Like the Julianas of the earlier versions, the Middle English Juliana makes no attempt to soften the hearts of her father and suitor. Just as her literary predecessors do, she too binds the "kempe of hell," her personal devil, when he comes to her cell in order to seduce her will. Unlike the others, however, she not only binds this devil—which seems quite reasonable under the circumstances—but she administers to him a beating equal in severity to those she has received, until he begins to shriek and holler.[27] Juliana's father has shown her no mercy; so, she tells "belial," she will show him none.[28] It is to Juliana's might, not to her goodness, that the devil finally yields, as he admits.[29] Her severity here seems directly proportionate to the temptation; the devil, representing part of herself, before his true nature is revealed, does indeed elicit more of a response from her than either her father or her suitor have done.

At first, Juliana seems a curious model for female conduct and female virtue in an age which found Mary's Mantle of Meekness emblematic of an ideal submission.[30] But the author's and the reader's approval of Juliana's pugnacity must be conditional. Her "unwomanliche" behavior is acceptable only under the influence of two competing fathers, as shown also in the life of St. Margaret, and given the sexual neutrality created by her virginal state, which is stressed by the author.

Juliana's "fleshliche feader," African, at the beginning of the work, is carefully separated from the father in heaven. As in fairy tales, where a child's ambivalence towards the parent may be represented by the figures of a good king and a wicked troll, the heroine's good feelings and bad feelings towards the father, her dependency and rebellion, are distinctly divided in the Middle English *Juliana*.[31] Juliana may struggle with her earthly father only if she is obedient to the benign father who makes his appearance in the first line of the work as the lord of love and of creation ("frumscheft"). Even if Juliana rebels and disproves African's boast that he will deliver his daughter over to Eleusius as a bride "þah hit hire unwil were" (though against her will), she submits to the will of the heavenly Father, in this case through identification with the passive but beloved Son.[32]

Furthermore, Juliana's virginity neutralizes her sexual identity. Saint Ambrose wrote that "she who does not believe is a woman and should be designated by the name of her bodily sex, whereas she who believes progresses to complete manhood, to the measure of the adulthood of Christ."[33] Within this system where souls are equal but the sexes are not, the woman may rid herself of her female attributes, "worldly name, gender of body, youthful seductiveness, and garrulousness of age," if she remains a virgin.[34] Vern L. Bullough draws attention to St. Jerome's unequivocal statement of the same idea:

> as long as woman is for birth and children, she is different from man as body is from soul. But if she wishes to serve Christ more than the world, then she will cease to be a woman and will be called man.[35]

It is no wonder then that the medieval redactor of *Iuliene* stresses the power of his heroine's virginity more than the Latin writers or Cynewulf do. The masculine-active traits of character she exhibits throughout the work would be unacceptable if she were not clearly virginal. That the Middle English writer should be more careful of this than the Anglo-Saxon points, I believe, to a greater and more stringent division—almost a polarization—between male and female identifications in the later period. Whatever the advantages of feudal civilization, the tribal egalitarianism of the Anglo-Saxons seems to have allowed for much more scope and strength in the female character.[36]

In the Middle English *Margaret* or *Marharete*, the alliterative prose version of which appears in two early thirteenth-century manuscripts,[37] the setting is pastoral; the heroine gentler, noble, and more appealing; and the conflicts in male/female identifications are more fully internalized, revealing an unexpected sophistication in the redactor. Whereas Juliana appears against the backdrop of the marketplace and always in the shadow of Imperial Rome, Margaret's setting is at once more detailed and less harsh. *Marharete* was a very popular life in the medieval period, and although one balks at the notion of an entertaining martyrdom, this legend seems to have been part of the literature of entertainment, as well as inspiration.[38] The good parent here is a much more powerful presence. Such a development might have been crucial in the legend's popular success, an expression of the workings, in fantasy at least, of father-daughter relations within a strictly patriarchal society.

The plot is much the same as that of *Iuliene*. A wicked would-be suitor lusts after a beautiful Christian maiden. He is a pagan, of course, and in anger at the rejection of his advances, he procedes to torture and torment the heroine, while he offers mercy if she will yield to his will. Margaret is also cast into prison, where she is tempted by a devil, this time in the form of a dragon. She too overcomes temptation, and she too is put to death for refusing to bend in her beliefs.

There are important differences in treatment between *Marharete* and *Iuliene*. Although the author begins with the formulaic naming of her "fleschliche feder," we find that Margaret is, at fifteen, an orphan, her mother "having gone the way all earthly men shall go."[39] This is a common yet significant fairy tale device: her mother dead, her "fleschliche feder" conveniently disappears, so that Margaret may explicitly project the image of the good father onto heavenly "drihtan," the Lord. In the prison scene, Margaret alludes to the two fathers in such a way as to clarify the division in the father image; to all earthly and heavenly things, she says to the Lord in her prayer,

> "You are the father; you foster helpless children. You are the wedded woman's well-being, the widow's provider, the maiden's prosperity. My own father, the father of my flesh, drove me away—his only daughter. . . ."[40]

Now the Lord must be both father and friend to her, she continues. Whereas Juliana identifies with male power in her active role, Margaret introjects the qualities of courage and love incorporated in the male godhead, identifies, that is, with the compassionate God the Father.

This distinction between the two figures is illustrated by their respective encounters with monster and dragon. Juliana is as cruel and merciless to the "kempe of helle" as her father and her suitor are to her. Margaret also wrestles with the dragon and casts him to the ground, but the narrator insists that what was most efficacious in defeating the dragon is the saint's prayer. Margaret herself declares that her strength comes from love. At the very moment when she defeats the dragon, who appears to symbolize a threatening phallic maleness, she celebrates her relation to the deity:

> "I am my Lord's lamb, and He is my shepherd. I am God's servant and his thrall that I may do all according to his dear will!"[41]

Although these images are scarcely original, they are important within this context for their pastoral yielding quality. These images offset the actual militancy of the saint. It is exactly at this point that she is rewarded by the appearance of a dove, promising her paradise: she has pleased the good father, whose benevolence prevails.

The narrative point of view in *Marharete* resembles the expository point of view in the *Ancrene Riwle* and *Hali Meidenhad*—works to be investigated shortly that manifest a benign paternalism—more than the point of view in *Iuliene*. The pastoral motifs and the presence of at least one female character, Margaret's foster mother, round out the world through which Margaret moves and indicate a healthier emotional climate.[42] Although the female is still identified with the passive, that very passivity the author presents as admirable. Margaret, unlike Juliana, is not held contemptible in her submissive moments. Although such a presentation bears problems also, it testifies to greater acceptance of gentleness and compassion.

It is to be noted that the dragon whom Margaret defeats finally salutes maidenhood because Christ was born of a maiden[43] and that Margaret, virginal herself, prays for suffering women who are not virgins—that is, for women in childbed:

> In that house where women suffer in childbirth, when they speak Thy name and my pain, Lord, kindly help them and hear their prayer; and in that house, allow to be born neither the misshapen of limb, nor the lame; nor the deaf and speechless nor any possessed by a devil.[44]

Mercy is seen here as part of the male godhead, and a woman may achieve virtue through identification with that aspect of the deity.

Stressing the merciful aspects of the patriarchal God and of His vicars on earth, however, accentuates great contradictions inherent in the notion of an omnipotent father. "The Second Nun's Tale" of *The Canterbury Tales* is the humane Chaucer's representative saint's life; in this recounting of the good works of St. Cecilia, the poet emphasizes the kindness of St. Urban, the Pope, depicted as an old man who christens, comforts, and encourages Cecilia, her virginal husband Valerian, and his brother Tiburce. St. Paul, too, who appears to Valerian in a vision, is old and kind.[45] The "Creatour of every creature" whom the Second Nun invokes in her prologue is described as "doghter of thy Sone," the "welle of mercy."[46] Logically enough, all these loving, nurturing, and naming and creating male figures are powerless: it is the pagan judge and "philosophre" who has the power. At the end of the tale, St. Urban must "prively" fetch the saint's body and bury it "by nyghte."[47] Moreover, the legend of St. Cecilia, her missionary success, as it were, is predicated upon her remaining a virgin, albeit a married woman. Although Chaucer deemphasizes this and concentrates on her persuasiveness instead, Cecilia's virginity is established by the given life as the first condition of her sanctity. Just as in *Iuliene* and *Marharete*, the heroine has to renounce her female identity—the possibility of bearing children—in order to achieve virtue.

Once more we see how the promise of certain thinkers, those who would grant women spiritual equality with men if the women remained virgins, cannot fulfill itself. Mary Daly writes of the dilemma into which patriarchal dogma plunged women. Women were supposed to have been by nature more physical and less spiritual than men; ergo, if women took it upon themselves to become as religious as men, they could be looked upon in part as going against nature, a grave error.[48] Indeed, some religious orders to which women flocked were suppressed on this very charge.[49] In the literature, fathers generally demonstrate a resistance to their daughters' entering into the religious life as if the religious vocations of their daughters would pose a threat to strict identifications in terms of gender.

The *Legendys of Hooly Wummen* of Osbern Bokenham confirms what one perceives as a pattern in the variously authored saints' lives. The *Legendys*, the product of a single sensibility given the materials of the *Legenda Aurea*, also provides information about both the redactor and his public.[50] Bokenham, an Augustinian friar, a Doctor of Divinity, and "a Suffolk man," born in 1392 or thereabout, Mary S. Serjeantson writes, had "a number of friends among patrons of literature in East Anglia," and was good enough to indicate the motivation for his work and the names of his patrons in the prologues to and commentary upon the legends themselves.[51] The extant information concerning Bokenham's patrons for each individual legend is as follows: Lady Bourchier requested the legend of Mary Magdalene in 1445; *St. Margaret* was written at the request of Thomas Burgh and then given to the nuns of a Cambridge convent; *St. Anne* was written for John Denston, his wife Katherine, and his daughter Anne between 1441 and 1463; *St. Katherine* is dedicated to both Katherine Denston and Katherine Howard; *St. Dorothy* was written for John Hunt and Isabel his wife; Agatha Flegge is mentioned in *St. Agatha*, and the legend of *St. Elizabeth* is associated with one Elizabeth de Vere.[52] Whether these legends furnished comfort or catechism or both to the women named one does not know, but the patronage granted Bokenham indicates that his presentation must have expressed the interests or ideals or fantasies of this class.

Even though mothers are present in Bokenham's legends, and in one case central,[53] it is for the most part the fathers who direct the course of their daughters' lives. Criticism of the fathers—even when they are pagans to be damned at their deaths as in *St. Margaret*—is minimal, although in almost every legend an older figure appears, a wicked judge or ruler, who is pitted against a benevolent heavenly father.[54] Submissiveness is stressed and in the life of St. Elizabeth explicitly celebrated, but the basic conflict once again arises. How active can a supposedly passive woman dare to be in her virtuous deeds and beliefs? How passive is it possible for a daughter to be if her first, most passionate relationship is with her father?

In Bokenham's *St. Cristyne*, for example, the author begins by stressing the worldliness of her father, his "degre . . . off the blode emperiall," and his pagan faith.[55] Cristyne comes from her parents, we are told, as a flower from a thorn bush; she is beautiful, prudent, and wise. She also has a mind of her own:

> Her only purpose was to love and serve
> The omnipotent lord of heaven and earth,
> But in the meantime she kept secret
> Her holy intention from her parents.[56]

Her father, Urban, realizes her great beauty, and curiously afraid of its consequences, builds a tower for the express purpose of keeping her there, safe from her many suitors. Within the tower, he sets up his golden idols for Cristyne to worship. The struggle of the heroine with her father begins in earnest:

> But no doubt this blessed Cristyne
> Was disposed in such a way
> Her father could not fathom or divine,
> For her heart was wholly applied
> To the service of God; therefore
> She would not sacrifice to idols
> As her father had bid her do,
> But in her heart she despised
> All his gods forged of silver and gold.[57]

Although Cristyne's maidens warn her that her father will be enraged by her disobedience, she remains steadfast. His first reproof is, in fact, gentle:

"Do you not know with what effort
And weeping, daughter, and what heaviness—
With great reverence and honor, too—
I purchased my gods' good will for you?
I hope it does not chance that for your
Unkindness they take vengeance on you;
Now step forward, and in humility
Sacrifice to them, I beg of you."[58]

A theological debate ensues, Urban questioning Cristyne's refusal to worship many gods, as it appears to him that she already worships three. The entire passage is a kind of naturalistic dialogue in which Urban displays great patience, and Cristyne great obstinacy. It culminates in Cristyne's complaining about her father's lack of intelligence:

"Now I perceive very well," said Cristyne,
"That you want wit and understanding,
And that you lack the influence of divine grace
For understanding the mystery of these things."[59]

Even at this point, Urban tolerates his daughter's behavior, and sends her the incense she has requested for her god. Only after she has willfully thrown his idols from the tower window does he become furious:

He slapped his daughter with force
Across her face, and spoke in the following way:
"Tell me where my gods are at once,
Before I really assail you with torments."[60]

To this Cristyne replies, in the manner of Juliana, that if his gods really exist they will speak for themselves, and so give evidence of their "godly dignite."[61]

Urban, now feeling compelled to employ force, beheads Cristyne's twelve maidens, the author's concession, perhaps, to the original material, and, like any medieval father, has Cristyne beaten.[62] She does not repent but instead taunts him during the beating.[63] This scene might have been problematic for Bokenham, as he makes it more complex than is his wont. Urban has his daughter bound and then goes home to his palace, where he falls upon the ground in sorrow and anguish because "he is so despised by his daughter."[64] Next, Cristyne's mother, whose actions I return to later, falls at Cristyne's feet and begs her to submit to her father's will. At this juncture, Cristyne utterly rejects her mother and disavows her natural parents:

> "I took my name from Christ my creator.
> He is my father, He is my mother, too.
> I will serve Him, I will worship Him
> That has assured me to have victory
> Over all of you who, blinded by idolatry,
> Do not worship the omnipotent God."[65]

Cristyne storms out of the palace, "forsaking" her mother and leaving her father so angry that he begins to "tremble and shake."[66] The next morning Urban finds the praetor, publicly disowns his daughter, and accuses her of irreverence, the equivalent of treason. Cristyne is tortured, and in her torture she turns to God. She states that Christ is her only "Father, and none but He."[67]

What is actually taking place in this domestic arena? Cristyne, we are told, is twelve years old, nubile but at a point when her sexual identity is in the balance. Bokenham's indication that Cristyne is emerging from childhood into adolescence makes her father's behavior comprehensible. Her father demonstrates ambivalence towards her marriageable state and prefers to shut her up in a tower rather than give her over to a young man. Her father is portrayed as attached to Cristyne, as we see in their discussions. At this stage, Cristyne is allowed some license in her behavior until she destroys the idols, an openly aggressive act. Such action defies the notion of gender identification and is therefore seen by the other characters as threatening. The mother begs her daughter to submit. Cristyne must disown her mother if she is to avoid passivity, as she does. Her acts of defiance and aggression are done in the name of God the Father and His Son, male personnae.

In this conflict, a major problem in medieval female hagiography emerges. The religious code has changed since pagan times, but the sexual code has not. The audience is Christian, but as patriarchal as the pagan Romans. Bokenham's treatment of Cristyne's break with her family reveals a subliminal understanding of the contradictions involved in the medieval version of the Freudian family romance. That he stresses Cristyne's submissiveness to God the Father also testifies to an intuitive grasp of the difficulties involved in strict identification by gender; Cristyne's strident and aggressive nature, translated to Heaven, might drive the Deity into a frenzy as well. The compensatory aggressiveness of male-identified women manifests itself in the depictions of many female saints—that Bokenham portrays in *St. Cristyne.*

It was undoubtedly safer to submit to the will of the father than to identify with his activity. Bokenham describes what might have been a model attitude. His St. Elyzabeth is father-oriented and yet submissive. When this holy woman reached marriageable age, we are told, "she was constrained by her father to marry":

> Being wedded seemed loathesome to her
> But she consented, not for lust
> Or the pleasure of her body,
> But because she would do her father's will,
> And because she might educate
> Her children, if God sent her fruit.[68]

Such an attitude in daughters cannot be accomplished by brute force alone. Bokenham's fathers resort to force only when persuasion, built upon dependency, fails. The psychological mechanism in a patriarchal context, responsible for the development of such a dependency, which we can see at work in the *Ancrene Riwle* and *Hali Meidenhad,* two tracts for women, is a rather simple one: "the father showers his daughter with affection and tenderness when she acts passive, helpless, and/or femininely seductive, but discourages her masculine and/or aggressive strivings."[69] Learning theorists believe a child will learn "to perform those behaviors which the parents reward":

in terms of the father's ability to reward particular behaviors it can be argued that he has a significant influence on his daughter's personality development. Paternal reinforcement of the girl's attempts to emulate her mother's behavior, and the father's general approval of the mother's behavior, seem particularly important.[70]

Some psychologists stipulate that the mother has "a primarily expressive relationship with both boys and girls"; the father, on the other hand,

> rewards his male and female children differently, encouraging instrumental behavior in his son and expressive behavior in his daughter. The father is supposed to be the principal transmitter of culturally based conceptions of masculinity and femininity.[71]

This would be especially true in a strictly patriarchal culture in which the father is respected, honored, worshipped, and obeyed. The principal tool for this kind of indoctrination is praise. The praise must come not only from an authority figure but also from an authority figure upon whom the daughter depends and in whom she trusts.

The author of the *Ancrene Riwle* seems to have been such a figure. The early thirteenth-century work went through many redactions, and it exists in a bewildering variety of manuscripts and editions.[72] Its dialect is difficult; and to compound the basic textual problems, there is some disagreement as to whether it was written originally in English or French.[73] Although it is not known whether the author himself revised the work, it is fairly certain that the original was composed at the behest of three female recluses.[74] The later versions are addressed to a larger community of women, and an attempt was made to present the material to religious persons of both sexes living within a religious community.[75] It is important to keep the behest of the original readers in mind. The anchoresses must have trusted the author, and a reading of the work makes such trust understandable. The author undertakes the counsel of the sisters in the external and internal rule of their lives with wit and charm, tolerance and knowledge.

Because the structure of the *Ancrene Riwle* is complicated, the language and thought rich, pithy, and intricate, it is difficult to take up only one strand of the work without distorting the rest of it. Clearly, the *Ancrene Riwle* does not conform to any set formula. I am therefore forced to pass over whatever does not pertain to the questions at hand—that is, whatever does not pertain immediately to what the author praises in women, to what is prohibited to women, and to how he makes some highly unpleasant doctrine acceptable to the young women in his charge, benevolent and fatherly priest that he is. The use and abuse of language, for example, is an important theme in the work as a whole, which is not surprising, as the author is a master of English prose. How does the author make the ban on preaching acceptable to women who are obviously highly skilled in verbalizing?

The author of the *Riwle*, as is his wont, puts old tropes to new uses. In this case he begins with the familiar comparison of Eve and Mary. He criticizes Eve for talking too much, but praises Mary at length and ingeniously for her sparing use of words:

> Eve had a long talk with the serpent in Paradise; she told him the entire lesson that God had delivered to her and to Adam so that the fiend understood immediately Eve's weakness. Our Lady, Saint Mary, acted entirely different. She didn't tell the angel any stories but asked as little as possible. So, yes, my dear sisters, follow the example of Our Lady, not the chattering Eve.[76]

Moreover, the author continues, Mary, to whom women in particular owe their prayers, "was of such light speech that nowhere in Holy Writ do we find her speaking except for four utterances."[77] Although she spoke but little, he emphasizes, "the words were heavy and had much power," so weighty in fact that through these words "God became Man."[78]

Having praised constraint or restraint in speech in general, the author moves on to St. Paul's injunction in particular. He admits that old women may sometimes preach: "Holy old anchoresses may sometimes do so, but it is not suitable for the young," the old being beyond gender, as it were.[79] He assures the young women that they are forbidden to preach not because of any intrinsic wickedness but because such an activity would lead them to sin unwittingly.[80] The tone is gentle here, the interpretation of Paul sympathetic, the final, delicately qualified prohibition meant for the protection of the young women themselves. The author has led his female readers to the traditional and orthodox position in which they are forbidden to preach, to lead, or to teach,[81] but through what the psychologist would call positive reinforcement. If the women follow these ever-so-gently worded commandments, both praise and love are to be theirs.

The author holds out his own and God the Father's approval again and again as he emphasizes the moral and physical fragility of women. Women's flesh is "brittle as any glass,"[82] and the anchoresses are easily tempted—or would be—by the sights of the world. The eye does more harm to women, so the wise think, than death.[83] The ear, as one might have suspected, is an equally dangerous organ, for through it loose and evil talk may penetrate the woman's defenses.[84] Anger, a particularly reprehensible trait that causes both men and women to lose their humanity and become bestial, when found in women is " wolfish"; should women let anger lead them from their better selves and purposes, they will become kin to the serpent, and not reap their reward of being "Christ's spouse."[85]

Of course, temptations of the flesh were to be shunned by all those attempting to lead a religious life. Anger, for example, was to be eschewed in the monastic orders as well as in communities of women. However, the softened tone, the earthy examples, and the assurances of protection are not to be found in rules for men. The author's kindliness makes the injunctions and sanctions much more acceptable, and the promise of being "Christ's spouse" makes obedience attractive—obedience, certainly, to a male figure, God or priest, and not to another woman.

The emphases in *Hali Meidenhad* are somewhat different, and the manner very different. This amazing work, reading in parts like a radical feminist tract in thirteenth-century English dialect, presents the woes of women—married women—in no uncertain terms. *Hali Meidenhad* was written to convince young women of the desirability of leading a religious life in an order removed from the world, thus leading a life outside the married state. The tone is urgent, the author's knowledge of the disadvantages for women in medieval matrimony and motherhood convincing, and his argument forceful. However, even this sympathetic male author's directive is this: maidens should give up their worldly, harsh male masters for a heavenly male master—undoubtedly more benign, but a master nonetheless.

To this end, the writer employs the authority and protectiveness of the paternal voice from the opening lines of the work:

> Listen to me, daughter, and look and give me your attention; forget your people and your father's house. David, the psalmwriter, speaks in the Psalms to God's spouse, that is, to each maiden who has taken a maiden's vows, and says: "Hear me, daughter! Behold, and give me your ear, and forget your folk and your father's house." . . . "Hear me, daughter," he says. "Daughter," he calls her, because he wishes her to understand that he lovingly teaches her about her life's love, as a father does his daughter.[86]

He presents a paradigm of the attitudes to be held by his readers and continues to describe at length this exemplary and comforting relationship.[87] He calls marriage slavery, "thralldom" in which the woman is "not free herself."[88] Leading the virginal life of a nun, however, the maiden will be not only "God's bride" but "his free daughter" for God, he says, "is both husband and father."[89] Thus, the writer offers his female audience not only erotic love but benevolent paternal care as well.

A problem emerges once more in regard to the feminine identifications of these virginal women, for the author presents motherhood in loathesome and degrading terms, so that there is a dilemma for women even in obedient virginity. As in Bokenham's *Lyf of S. Cristyne*, it seems that a repudiation of the mother or of motherhood itself is required. For what does the author of *Hali Meidenhad* tell these women about bearing children? In the first place, the woman must be contaminated in the sexual act; in the bearing itself, he says, "is heavyness";[90] in the birthing, a drain of strength and sometimes death. Moreover, the child brings with it more "care than bliss, and namely to the mother."[91] If the child is misbegotten, as it sometimes is, and "lacks one of his limbs"[92] or has some other defect, "it will be painful for her" since any defect in the child will be attributed to her.[93] And yet if the child is well at birth, the mother will have nothing but care that the child will be harmed, or that one of them, the mother or the child, will lose the other.[94]

Also, this writer warns the young women, you will be very sick when you are pregnant (no jest, of course, in medieval times). Your complexion will be green, your eyes will be dull, and "your brains turning, your head will sorely ache."[95] The swelling belly will be "bulging with water" and there will be "heaviness in each limb."[96] There will be much wailing; "the mouth is bitter," disliking all that is chewed; and whatever food is taken in this fashion, without desire, is cast right out again.[97]

The most distinct of feminine functions, then, that of giving birth to a child, is presented as sorrowful, sickening, and disgusting in the extreme. A woman may achieve freedom and dignity only "as God's free daughter and His Son's spouse," not as a mother—not even as a mother of men.[98] Here, again, is the denigration of female creativity. Given this outlook, the woman can identify either with her own mother's degradation in the bearing of children or, as a virgin, identify with and acquiesce to her father's power. This is not a very happy choice, of course, and must have proven itself, whichever was chosen, a heavy heritage, an iron dowry.

NOTES

1. F. J. Furnivall, ed., *Hali Meidenhad* (New York: Greenwood Press, 1969), p. 53: "Godes fre dohter, & his sones spuse."

2. M. Anthony Hewson, *Giles of Rome and the Medieval Theory of Conception* (London: The Athlone Press, 1975), p. 69. *Also see* chapter 1.

3. Frederick Engels, *The Origin of the Family, Private Property and the State,* ed. Eleanor Burke Leacock (New York: International Publishers, 1972), pp. 125–46.

4. Maurice Valency, *In Praise of Love* (New York: Farrar, Straus and Giroux, 1975), p. 60.

5. Dorigen is the loving wife of Chaucer's "The Franklin's Tale" in *The Canterbury Tales*; *Sir Orfeo* is an early Middle English version of the Orpheus and Eurydice legend.

6. For a time they could even be forced into marriages; *see* Roberta Frank, "Marriage in Twelfth and Thirteenth Century Iceland," *Viator* 4 (1973): 473–84. *Also see* H. S. Bennett, *The Pastons and Their England* (London: Cambridge University Press, 1922), "The Business of Marriage" and "Marriages for Sale," pp. 27–36.

7. Charles Brenner, *An Elementary Textbook of Psychoanalysis* (Garden City, N.Y.: Doubleday, 1966), pp. 44–9.

8. Doris Mary Stenton, *English Society in the Early Middle Ages* (London: Penguin, 1951), pp. 73–5; *see also* Bennett, *The Pastons and Their England*, p. 48, on Margery Paston's being unable to get a sufficient amount for her dowry from her father, even with her mother also having "laboured the matter."

9. The tendency to identify with the powerful father is part of the phenomenon psychologists call identification with the oppressor.

10. *See* Joseph M. McCarthy, *Humanistic Emphases in the Educational Thought of Vincent of Beauvais* (Leiden: E. J. Brill, 1976), pp. 136–42, on the education of women; *see also* Philippe Ariès, *Centuries of Childhood* (New York: Knopf, 1962), pp. 297–98, on the education of girls.

11. S.R.T.O. d'Ardenne, ed. (London: E.E.T.S., 1961). I refer to the Bodley text from this edition throughout.

12. Finally, a beheading; most female saints, rescued from boiling oil, beatings, and other tortures, succumb to this end, possibly indicating symbolic castration.

13. Such a double message appears in the tales of Jeanne d'Arc, of course, who proved herself superior to men at their own game: war.

14. C. W. Kennedy, trans., *The Legend of St. Juliana* (Princeton, N.J.: The University Library, 1906), intro., p. 1. This text includes both the Latin and the Anglo-Saxon versions.

15. Ibid., p. 3.

16. Ibid., pp. 7–8.

17. *See* Eleanor Como McLaughlin, "Equality of Souls, Inequality of Sexes," in *Religion and Sexism: Images of Women in the Jewish and Christian Traditions*, ed. Rosemary Radford Ruether (New York: Simon and Schuster, 1974), pp. 213–66.

18. Kennedy, *St. Juliana*, pp. 8 and 21.

19. In entire poems as well, such as *Exodus* and *Judith*.

20. Stanley Rubin, *Early English Medicine* (New York: Barnes and Noble, 1974), pp. 19–42, discusses the archeological evidence of male/female division of labor.

21. *See*, for example, the Finnsburg Fragment in *Beowulf*.

22. *See* the translation of C. W. Kennedy in *Medieval English Literature*, ed. J. B. Trapp (New York: Oxford University Press, 1973), 11. 596–9 and 11. 1061–80; also, 1110–25.

23. *See* Frank, "Marriage in Twelfth and Thirteenth Century Iceland," and John T. Noonan, Jr., "Power to Choose," *Viator* 4 (1973): 419–57, on forced marriages.

24. Kennedy, *St. Juliana*, p. 34.

25. That is to say, unnatural.

26. *Iuliene*, p. 9.

27. Ibid., p. 43.

28. Ibid., p. 43.

29. Ibid., p. 45: "O þe mihte of meiðhad as þu art iwepnet to weorrin aȝein us" and "þe hauest þin hehe seotel o meiðhades mihte."

30. On the Mantle of Meekness, *see* William Patterson Cumming, ed., *The Revelations of Saint Birgitta* (London: E.E.T.S., 1929), pp. 100–01.

31. *See* Bruno Bettelheim, *The Uses of Enchantment* (New York: Alfred Knopf, 1976), pp. 66–73.

32. *Iuliene*, p. 27: Juliana echoes the words of Christ on the cross: "Mi feader & mi moder. . . habbe forsake me." This also constitutes the only reference to a mother in the work.

33. *See* Vern L. Bullough, "Medieval Medical and Scientific Views of Women," *Viator* 4 (1973): 499; this is from the *Expositio Evangelis secundum Lucam*.

34. *See* McLaughlin, "Equality of Souls," and Bullough, "Views of Women," p. 499.

35. Bullough, "Views of Women," p. 499.

36. And thus produced the great abbesses and female religious of the period such as Hilde and Waldeburga.

37. Frances M. Mack, ed., *Seinte Marharete: þe Meiden ant Martyr* (Oxford: E.E.T.S., n.d.). I refer to Mack's edition throughout.

38. Ibid., intro., p. xi.

39. Ibid., p. 5.

40. Ibid., p. 19: "þu art foster and feder to helplese children. þu art iweddedes weole, & widewene warant, & meidenes mede. . . Min ahne fleschliche feder dude & draf me awei, his anlepi dohter."

41. Ibid., p. 29: "Ich am mi lauerdes lomb, & he is min hirde. Ich am godes þeowe & his þrel to don al þet his deore wil is!"

42. *See* Joan M. Ferrante's final chapter in *Woman as Image in Medieval Literature: From the Twelfth Century to Dante* (New York: Columbia University Press, 1975).

43. *Marharete*, p. 28.

44. Ibid.: "'I þet hus þer wummon pineð o childe, sone se ha munneð þi nome & mi pine, lauerd; lauered hihendliche help hire & her hire bene; ne i þe hus ne beð iboren na mis-limet bearn, nowðer halt ne houeret, nowðer dumbe ne deaf ne ideruet of deofle."

45. *See* F. N. Robinson, ed., *The Works of Geoffrey Chaucer* (Boston: Houghton-Mifflin, 1957), pp. 207–13, and 11.200–17 in particular.

46. Ibid., p. 207, 11. 35–49.

47. Ibid., p. 213, 11. 547–50.

48. *See Beyond God the Father: Towards a Philosophy of Women's Liberation* (Boston: Beacon Press, 1973); Daly calls these contradictory demands "double-binding."

49. *See* Ferrante, *Woman as Image*, on the Cistercian order, for example.

50. In the edition of Mary S. Serjeantson (London: E.E.T.S., 1938), which I refer to hereafter.

51. Ibid., intro., p. xii.

52. Ibid., intro., pp. xx–xxi.

53. *Lyf of S. Lucye*; ibid., pp. 244–57.

54. That these are authority figures should not be overlooked; in *Marharete*, too, Olibrius, her "suitor," is a sheriff.

55. Serjeantson, *Legendys*, p. 58.

56. Ibid., p. 59.

57. Ibid., p. 59.

58. Ibid., p. 62.

59. Ibid., p. 62.

60. Ibid., p. 65.

61. Ibid., p. 65.

62. *See* Haskell, "The Paston Women on Marriage in Fifteenth Century England," *Viator* 4 (1973): 459–71; also, Ariés, *Centuries of Childhood,* pp. 258–62.

63. Serjeantson, *Legendys*, p. 66.

64. Ibid., p. 66.

65. Ibid., p. 67.

66. Ibid., p. 67.

67. Ibid., p. 69.

68. Ibid., p. 263.

69. Henry B. Biller, *Father, Child and Sex Role: Paternal Determinants of Personality Development* (Lexington, Mass.: D.C. Heath & Co., 1971), p. 106.

70. Ibid., p. 106.

71. Ibid., p. 107.

72. *See* J. R. R. Tolkien, *"Ancrene Wisse* and Hali Meidenhad," *Essays and Studies* 14 (1929): 104–20; also the introduction to his edition of *Ancrene Wisse* (London: E.E.T.S., 1962).

73. *See* Bertha Grattan Lee, *Linguistic Evidence for the Priority of the French Text* (The Hague: Mouton, 1974); also, Janet Grayson, *Structure and Imagery in Ancrene Wisse* (Hanover: The University Press, 1974).

74. *See* E. J. Dobson, ed., *The English Text of the Ancrene Riwle* (London: Oxford University Press, 1972), p. x. I use Dobson's text hereafter.

75. In the text edited from MS. Titus D. xviii.

76. *Ancrene Riwle*, p. 54:

Eue heold iparais long tale wið þe neddre. talde him al þe lecun þe god hefde ired hire & adam of þen god swa þe feont vnder stont anan richt hire wacnesse. . . ure lauedi seinte marie dude al an oðer wiðe. ne talde ha þe engel nan tale. ach askede him scheortliche þing þ ha ne cuðe. ȝe mine leue sustren folloȝeð ure lauedi naut þe chakele eue.

77. Ibid., p. 54: Mary "wes of se lute speche. þ nowhere in ahali write ne finde we þ ha spec butten four siðen. ach for þe selt speche þe wordes weren heurie."

78. Ibid., p. 54: The words "hefden muche machte. . . soo god bi com mon."

79. Ibid., p. 58: "Halie alde ancres hit maȝe don summes weis, ach hit ne limppeð naut to ȝunge."

80. Ibid., p. 58.

81. Ibid., p. 58: "*docere.*"

82. Ibid., p. 128: "Wummones flesch . . . bruchele as is eni gles."

83. Ibid., p. 53.

84. Ibid., p. 72.

85. Ibid., p. 98.

86. *Hali Meidenhad*, p. 3:

Audi, filia, & uide & inclina aurem tuam; & obliviscere populam tuam, &
domum patris tui. Dauid, þ salmwrihte, spekeð i þe sauter toward godes
soyse, þat is, euch meiden þat haueð meidene þeawes, & seið: "Her me,
dohter! Bihald, & buh þin eare, & for3et to folc & tine fader hus." . . . "Iher
me, dohter," he seið. "Dohter," he clepeð hire, for-þi þat ha understonde,
þat he hir liues luue luueliche leareð, ase fader ah his dohter."

87. Ibid., pp. 3–4.
88. Ibid., p. 7.
89. Ibid., p. 7: The maiden is "godes brude" and "his freo dohter—for ba to
3ederes ha is."
90. Ibid., p. 46.
91. Ibid., p. 46: More "care þen blisse, nomeliche to þe moder."
92. Ibid., p. 46: "wonti eni of his limen."
93. Ibid., p. 46.
94. Ibid., p. 46.
95. Ibid., p. 49: "þi breines turnunge þin heued ake sare."
96. Ibid., p. 49.
97. Ibid., p. 50.
98. Ibid., p. 53.

NATURAL MOTHERS: THE POWERLESS MIRROR

"Both nuns and mothers worship images."
—*W.B. Yeats*[1]

Robert Briffault writes in *The Mothers* of bonds between women and between mothers and daughters that seem to him to antedate the codes of patriarchal society and govern the behavior of women towards each other.[2] Although Briffault's work has been discredited, its historicity being very questionable,[3] the author's grasp of what exacerbated rivalry between women remains firm. He posits that the tensions between mother and daughter originate in economic and social dependency upon men. Although the existence of a true matriarchy now seems improbable at any time in world history, Briffault's conjecture that when women themselves had the means of survival at their disposal mothers and daughters need not have been rivals for the love of husband or father is a perceptual truth, independent of history.[4] Beneath the popular representation of mothers functioning as the primary agents, for example, of a repressive sexual order, another image lies, one which indicates that the bonds between mother and daughter have never really fallen away but are present in the worst of times, although made manifest in darkness and in secrecy.

No one can deny that rivalry exists between mothers and daughters, and no one can deny that mothers have indeed been repressive, tyrannical, and the perpetuators of the patriarchal modes. Andrea Dworkin writes powerfully of the damage to the mother-daughter bond that a custom such as Chinese footbinding must have wreaked:

What must the Chinese daughter/child have felt toward the mother who bound her feet? What does any daughter/child feel toward the mother who forces her to do painful things to her own body? The mother takes on the role of enforcer: she uses seduction, command, all manner of force to coerce the daughter to conform to the demands of the culture. It is because this role becomes the dominant role in the mother-daughter relationship that tensions and difficulties between mothers and daughters are so often unresolvable.[5]

Certainly, if "the father's general approval of her mother's behavior" is crucial in a daughter's development, it is no wonder that mothers have unwittingly abetted repressive patriarchal goals simply by providing their daughters with models of fear and submissiveness.[6] Romantic love, or a perversion of it, may have in this way—that is, in the pleasing of the male—served to weaken the bonds between and among women.[7] In the struggle for the male's protection and affection, in the struggle for survival, who can say that mothers and daughters have always seen their way clear to their basic allegiance?

Of course, rivalry and repression do show themselves in the literature of the Middle Ages when mothers are depicted with their daughters. What is surprising, however, is the degree to which love, support, and empathy persist in a period when a semblance of unity among women was suspect and punishable.[8] Dame Juliana of Norwich, for example, describes the mothering function thus:

> The Mother's service is nearest, readiest, and safest: for it is most of truth. . . .The kindly, loving Mother who understandeth and knoweth the need of her child, she keepeth it most tenderly, as the nature and condition of motherhood will. And as it waxeth in age, she changeth her method but not her love. And when it is grown older, she allows it to be chastened in breaking down the vices, to make the child receive virtues and graces.[9]

Dame Juliana is writing here of an idealized mother, of course, not attempting an individual portrait. Bokenham, curiously enough, presents a passionately loving mother in a more detailed way, in the *Lyf of S. Cristyne*:

> When Cristyne's mother had plainly heard
> How she had suffered such torments
> At the hands of her father, like a madwoman,
> Out of her wits with fear,

She rent her clothes, strewed ashes
On her head, and in that guise
Went to the prison where Cristyne was.
Falling to the ground and piteously weeping,
She told her daughter her feeling:
"O daughter Cristyné, have mercy on me,
Your wreched mother, for I have only you
And no one else, that can be the light
Of my eye! Think, daughter, how I—
For ten months—bore you in my body
And how I with great pain brought you
Into this world!"[10]

That Cristyne's mother is helpless and cannot defy her husband is to be expected; that she begs the girl to give in comes as no surprise; but that her grief is like that of a madwoman, that she fears for her daughter "as a wood woman," as if crazed, indicates the existence of passions in the particular. Bokenham's plodding verse lacks Dame Juliana's mystical transports, and his dialogues are far from imaginative; but his domestic scenes have a certain authenticity, given what seems to be his very literal mind. Juliana's caring mother might have been invented; Bokenham's frantic and fearful one must have been suggested by some observed behavior in reality.

The mother-daughter relationship depicted in the *Lyf of S. Cristyne* is of interest not only for the passionate outburst of the fearful mother but also for the complications that follow it. Cristyne utterly rejects her mother, and the breasts that have nurtured her.[11] "Do not call me daughter," she commands, and as she takes her leave announces, "here I forsake you."[12] Cristyne's mother has urged her to submit and bend to the father, to give up her beliefs, her selfhood. The mother urges this in an attempt to protect her daughter, but Cristyne is thereby forced to disown her mother, as if she sees her own potential passivity in her mother's behavior and must flee from it, or banish it, as it were. "The daughter who rejects the cultural norms enforced by the mother is forced to a basic rejection of her own mother," Dworkin remarks,[13] and this we see in Bokenham's saint's life. Moreover, the rejected mother returns to the father, telling him everything that has transpired. He, at this juncture, is so enraged that he decides to set the law upon Cristyne.[14] Cristyne, in rejecting her mother and her mother's role, is threatening the structure of the patriarchy, but in doing so she has alienated her mother, who betrays Cristyne and allies herself with the father instead.

A different resolution appears in Bokenham's *Lyf of S. Lucye*. In this legend, Lucye's father has died before Lucye has come of age and before the action begins, leaving Lucye and her mother outside the framework of the traditional patriarchal family unit.[15] Lucye and Eutyce, the mother, are allied in their wisdom and goodness and allied in their way of life. When Eutyce is stricken with dysentery, the daughter mothers her: nurses her, comforts her, and takes her to the tomb of Saint Agatha. We note that the saint, too, is female, as this legend concerns itself with women in a women's world. Lucye urges her mother to touch the tomb in good faith, promising her that if she does so she will be cured.[16] Saint Agatha then appears to Lucye in a dream, and indicates the terms of Eutyce's recovery. These Lucye relates to her mother:

> "Mother, be happy and of good cheer
> For there is to be relief for your misery,
> And you are to be cured of your sickness.
> Therefore I ask of you, for the goodness
> Of her through whose prayers you are made whole,
> That in no manner hereafter, neither in earnest
> Nor in game, will you present me with
> An earthly husband, nor that you desire
> Ever of my body that it produce fruit
> Through fleshly corruption.
> But all the things which you
> Would have given me if I were to give my virginity
> To a mortal corruptor, give me joining
> To the conservator and keeper of my virginity:
> Jesus Christ, who is forever blessed!"[17]

In other words, Lucye's mother will be cured of her sickness if Lucye is allowed to remain a virgin. The two women must abjure the male world completely if they are to help and support each other.

The mother agreeing to dispose of her wealth in the way Lucye thinks fit, the two go about doing acts of charity in peace until the man to whom Lucye has been betrothed appears; he has heard what they are doing, and he considers the distribution of Eutyce's money to be the squandering of his property. He questions Lucye's nurse, but she—providing another example of the solidarity of women in this legend—lies about the matter, telling the would-be husband that the two women are investing the money. When he learns the truth, that they are in fact spending their fortune in "almes-dedes," he decides to take revenge—or force Lucye's hand—by reporting her to the Roman court. As Lucye will not sacrifice to the pagan gods, the judge devises a cure for what he views as her obstinacy:

> "Right away I shall ordain
> A remedy to drive the Holy Ghost
> From you; to the brothel
> You shall be led."[18]

Lucye's punishment, then, is to be a kind of continuous rape. She is not beaten by this judgement, however, and claims that she would not be sinning if sent to the brothel since women are raped against their will. With the help of angels, she stands rooted to the spot; not even oxen can drag her off. The judge, astounded by her immobility, accuses her of witchcraft, the traditional accusation against strong women-centered women.[19]

In this legend, then, men are intruders and enemies. If, at the time of her daughter's martyrdom, Eutyce is not present in the flesh, the significance of the many mother-daughter scenes remains. The love and loyalty between the two women, made possible in the first place by their removal from the patriarchal family unit, threatens male society in its most basic concerns and values: property, in the case of Lucye's former suitor, and obedience to authority, in the case of the judge. But such a mother-daughter bond can exist, the legend suggests, only if Lucye remains unmarried, a virgin, as if this tie would not be possible once an involvement with men in the patriarchal world should occur.

If women within the religious community experienced some degree of autonomy—and returning to this we shall see that they did—outside that community their lives were so intertwined with those of men that it is difficult to discover the individual existences of women, aside from records of financial transactions or other legal matters. Moreover, a very strong sense of decorum precluded quotidian observations in certain literary forms such as the romance: one does not know, for example, what Palymoun and Arcite in "The Knight's Tale" ate for breakfast, how many people served it, and whether these were women or men. Whenever quotidian events are mentioned or whenever earthy details are given, the effect is one of charm—as the detail is so unexpected—or satire.[20] Whether the fact that literature was predominantly a male domain has to do with the peculiar disembodiment of certain literary forms or not—women being identified with the physical[21]—the lack of detail effectively obliterates much that we might otherwise have known about women of the court, for example. Even Chaucer, who provides more naturalistic detail than most medieval authors—consider Gower or Malory—still did not create in what could in any way be called a natural-istic tradition. Fortunately, another extant body of work does relate to secular life, variously designated and called by one scholar the "literature of entertainment."[22] To this body of work belong the anonymous lyrics and riddles, the tall tales, some satires such as the French *Renard the Fox* cycle, many of the plays that, although religious in themes and didactic purposes, manage to depict daily life, and the *fabliaux*. Writing of this kind Philippe Verdier compares to the marginal drawings of select medieval manuscripts and to the demons and gargoyles of medieval cathedrals; he claims that these reveal a world of "choses à anvers," the expression of a kind of medieval counterculture that admitted ideas, images, and realities banned from the more formal genres.[23] More women appear in this popular literature, and although they are frequently made the butt of, as Eileen Power puts it, a "secular antifeminism as brutal as anything which the Fathers of the Church had propounded,"[24] we may at least discern something in these works about the lives of women. Although one must be careful not to read this material too literally, paticularly the *fabliaux*, comic tales the audience of which is still the subject of debate,[25] the family is a real entity in the popular material, the women present along with the clank of coins and the cackle of hens.

While scenes depicting mothers and daughters are not exactly plentiful, the secular and quotidian concerns of these works dictate that some appear. A passage from a thirteenth-century tale in English called *Dame Sirith*, the central figure of which is an aged crone and go-between, presents us with the old mother complaining about the metamorphosis of her daughter into a dog (!).[26]

"I had a fair and noble daughter—
a fairer one you couldn't see—
who had a very gentlemanly husband—
no nobler any man than he.
My daughter loved him all too well,
and this is why I grieve:
one day he went out of the house—
and this was how my daughter was ruined—
for he had an errand out of town;
There came a haughty, shaven cleric,
and declared his love to my daughter
who wouldn't do his bidding.
He couldn't have his way with her
in anything that he desired.
Then this cleric cast a spell
and turned my daughter into a bitch.
This is my daughter of whom I speak:
for pity of her my heart breaks."[27]

The ludicrousness of this situation should not obscure its meaning. Dame Sirith tells of a reverse Circe situation in which the young woman, her daughter, has been turned into a beast because she acted out of higher motives. There are several layers of rather heavy-handed satire here, of course: if this *fabliau* emerged from the aristocracy, then pretensions to courtly behavior on the part of the burgher class are being mocked; if Dame Sirith was a production of the students, as current opinion has it, then the satire on the clergy seems most salient.[28] Whatever the class satire, Dame Sirith's monologue presents an ironic comment on the plight of women, for even when a woman acts correctly and morally, she is still likely to become the object of male whim and vindictiveness. The mother, for all her cleverness as a go-between and for all her scheming, is helpless in the face of this vindictiveness. The only thing she can do, both literally and figuratively, is to keep her daughter on a leash.

Of Chaucer's two famous *fabliaux*, "The Reeve's Tale" affords a brief glimpse of the life of plain people. The tale concerns the attempts of two students to get even with a miller and his wife for having cheated them of their grain and for having caused them no end of trouble in the process. In terms of the *fabliaux* tradition, the bloodless revenge could take only one form: seduction—perhaps too polite a word—of the miller's daughter. In the same night, one of the students takes the miller's wife also, by ruse. Thus, mother and daughter are placed in the same category, and it is the miller himself, rather than his wife, who is angry about his daughter having been "swived":

> "Ah, false traitor, false cleric," he said,
> "You shall be dead, by God's dignity—
> Who dare be so bold as to disparage
> My daughter, who is come of such lineage?"[29]

Although one must bear in mind that this is a *fabliau* and not an attempt to describe the people of the third estate realistically, the action of the plot is revealing in regard to the domestic relations of the miller, his wife, and his daughter. The miller blames neither his wife nor his daughter but threatens the two students; his wife is not presented as blaming the daughter, and the daughter—unlike the mother—has been ready and willing to take the young cleric into her bed. Though it would be unsafe to make much of this, given the zaniness of the genre, the sexual scruples generating mother-daughter conflict in later eras seem to be lacking here. One wonders whether—in the peasant, artisan, or merchant class— women were more permissive in regard to their daughters' honor or if, as in this *fabliau*, both mothers and daughters were simply exposed to the same hazards, thus precluding harsh judgements of daughters' mores.

This lack of harshness on the part of the mother is shown—this time at length and somewhat higher on the social scale, among the gentry— in *The Book of the Knight of the Tour-Landry*.[30] In form, this fifteenth-century work is related to a number of books on deportment, but it differs from many of them in emphasizing the theoretical bases of the rules therein.[31] Indeed, it has been called a "treatise on social ethics,"[32] and it is more self-conscious than the other works in that its author, Geoffrey, has as his explicit goal the education of his three daughters.

At the time he wrote this book, Geoffrey was a widower; he incorporates the advice of his late wife, the mother of these three young women, in his thesis. While Geoffrey himself is not above narrating some stories of women punished for various infringements of his code,[33] the mother herself is presented by him as gentle and charming, and her advice to her daughters is of a different quality from Geoffrey's own.

There are even certain ironic poignancies in his portrait of her in relation to the girls as, for example, when Geoffrey writes of the mother trying to protect her daughters from the well-meaning but ill-founded advice of her husband—and from the carelessness of all men. "Ye say," she tells her husband,

> "and so do all other men, that a lady or damsel is the better worth when she loveth par amours, and that she be the more gay and of fair manner and countenance, and how she shall do great alms in esbatement [play] of lords and of fellows, in a language much common. . . .
>
> But these words cost to them but little to say for to get the better and sooner the grace and good will of their paramours. For of such words, and others much marvellous, many a one useth full oft. But, howbeit that they say that "For them and their love they do it," in good faith, they do it only for to enhance themself and for to draw unto them the grace and vainglory of the world."[34]

The mother's skepticism in regard to the sexual blandishments of men is presented as being much more down-to-earth than the attitude of the father, who seems to be preoccupied throughout with the question of obedience, at any rate. She also invokes a kind of sexual solidarity that he, of course, cannot call upon:

> "Therefore, I charge you, my fair daughters, that in this matter ye believe not your father. But I pray you that ye hold yourself cleanly and without blame, and that ye be not amorous, for many reasons which I shall rehearse unto you."[35]

She goes on to say in several ways that men are deceivers.[36] Here the mother is shown to be counselor and confidante; she seems to be concerned with protecting her daughters through the sharing of her wisdom and experience. Instead of holding forth on morality—as well she might have, Christian morality looking askance at sexual curiosity and "solace" —she simply warns the young women of the dangers to themselves, to their trust and integrity, in amorous situations.

Geoffrey presents his lady as at least somewhat influential in regard to her daughters' future conduct. In many romances, however, natural mothers are not even presented as giving advice; the more aristocratic the class, the less, it seems, the mother's presence and influence manifest themselves.

The most courtly of poets, Chretien de Troyes, in *Erec and Enide*, presents a mother whose only contribution to the action is to weep in sympathy! The mother of Enide is depicted as a totally pliant and passive creature. Mother and daughter enter this romance together as they emerge from a workroom. I believe that we are allowed to see the mother because Enide's father is simply a vavasour, and not of the very highest social standing. The vavasour himself—as Erec's host—instructs his daughter in how to treat the noble guest and tells Enide to take Erec by the hand and to lead him upstairs. What has the mother done since she emerged from the workroom?

> The lady had gone before and prepared the house. She had laid embroidered cushions and spreads upon the couches, where they all three sat down— Erec with his host beside him, and the maiden opposite.[37]

The mother sets the scene but does not participate in it. Throughout the entire conversation, which is considerable, between Erec and Enide's father, she does not utter a sound. At the conclusion of the scene and of the evening, Enide's father bestows her on Erec while the maiden "sat quiet" but "was very happy and glad," we are told, "that she was betrothed to him, because he was valiant and courteous."[38]

If Enide's attitude seems passive, let us regard that of her mother: of her we only know that she "weeps for joy."[39] So, too, at another point— when Erec carries off his bride-to-be—the mother participates in this minimal fashion:

> Then the Count kisses Erec and his niece, and commends them both to merciful God. Her father and mother, too, kiss them again and again, and could not keep back their tears: at parting, the mother weeps, the father and the daughter, too. For such is love and human nature, and such is affection between parents and children.[40]

Or so it is in patriarchal societies. This mother can do nothing except weep, first in joy and then in sorrow.

But what if literary conventions are blocking the view of what actually transpired? Those conventions in and of themselves reveal attitudes towards natural mothers. Chretien wrote in good part for women, and for rather powerful ladies at that.[41] Was the court poet to portray these ladies' mothers realistically? Or would powerful women wish to deny their experience as daughters? When natural mothers appear in the romances, they are usually weeping in helpless sympathy, as in *Floris and Blancheflour*.[42] The repeated action might well contain at least some symbolic truth, but a poet writing for the powerful most likely would not dwell upon reminders of impotence. To discuss motherhood and mothering was in the first place too physical a subject for the romance genre. Would it not also remind the ladies of an aspect of their lives they would not wish to see within their looking-glasses, themselves as mothers or daughters, with the accompanying intimations of helplessness?

The Paston Letters serve both to complicate and to illuminate this issue.[43] These letters, "dating principally from the fifteenth century," Ann S. Haskell writes, "stand in distinct contrast to the popular notions of well-born medieval women, deduced from such models as romance heroines."[44] The major female letter-writers, Margaret Paston and her mother-in-law Agnes, "are seen as practical individuals of real social and economic power in their later lives."[45] Furthermore, toward the end of her excellent article, Haskell remarks that the "intractable attitudes of medieval mothers toward their daughters are the rule, rather than the exception, judging by the correspondence before us."[46] She observes that severe punishments were commonly inflicted on children of either sex, that displays of affection seem to have been few, and that women who gave birth to daughters

> lived with a double anguish, originally for having disappointed their fathers, and subsequently for having been the instruments of revealing their husbands' weakness. The bitterness of medieval women seems never to have reached greater depths than in dealing with their daughters, *with whom some degree of self-identification must have been present.*[47]

All of what Haskell has to say may indeed be true—although the evidence is not overwhelming[48]—and yet not efface literary evidence yielding what appears to be a different image. It seems to me that the two images both pertain to the identical phenomenon, but that poetry displays the underlying emotional structures of a given historical reality, whereas with historical documents one must deduce the emotional structure from the features.

The Paston women were able to do certain things—write as well as read, for example, and control large estates while their husbands were absent—[49] which the majority of people were not able to do. It is a commonplace that women of wealth have had more power than the poor of either gender, but simply because Elizabeth I exercised power we cannot deduce that the status of women as women was elevated thereby. Women who have exercised power in the male world have tended to be male-identified in their goals, and the Pastons, I believe, were no exceptions. Of Margaret Paston's numerous pregnancies, Haskell writes:

> This status. . . would not have been without its positive value; her child-bearing was the obvious and ultimate statement of femininity, and could have prevented accusations that her behavior was, on occasion, unfeminine, masculine or, in some instances, possibly even hysterical. It is interesting to consider that religious women who, like Margaret Paston, managed large estates, had no apparent need to demonstrate their femininity, since, as Vern Bullough reminds us, they had attained the status of males.[50]

Bullough is citing the writings of the Church Fathers who recognized male and female but not really neutral or nonmale status.[51] Moreover, as Eileen Power pointed out, the only soft spot in Margaret's hard heart seems to have been for her husband.[52] That is to say, not only did the lady do a great deal that was generally held to be in the male dominion, but she seems to have been male-centered in her affections as well. To the extent that she had departed from female status, then, her daughters must have provoked intense and compensatory responses. The daughter who internalizes the values of the patriarchy, Dworkin writes, maintains a "subterranean" form of "anger and resentment. . . channeled against her own female offspring as well as her mother."[53]

Margaret Paston's cruel attempts at subjugating her daughters reveal her profound ambivalence towards herself as a woman and towards woman's role. In an extension of a "Do what I say and not what I do" code, which her daughters did not seem to heed,[54] Margaret Paston attempted to inculcate in her female offspring the medieval ideal of submission, even if heads were broken in the process.[55] Her guilt and ambiguity in relation to her own status must have been tremendous and may have added the extra degree of punitive fury Margaret demonstrated, for example, when Elizabeth refused to marry the husband Margaret had chosen for her.

Mothers as mothers were powerless; only in her role of substitute father was Margaret Paston able to make decisions or try to arrange and force the events of her daughters' lives. Her hatred for the passive-sympathetic mode of conduct shows itself in the ferocity of her attempts to make her daughters obey.

It is interesting that these women modeled themselves along the lines indicated by their mothers' behavior, rather than along the lines indicated by their mothers' behests. Haskell, though raising a fascinating question, overlooks an obvious answer. She asks "how medieval girls became adult women of such self-assurance as the Pastons":

> Constant subordination surely must have produced some repressed human beings, but for those from whom we have self-documentation, a young womanhood of bending to the will of elders was apparently thought of as a period of double-entry bookkeeping; those who could survive such subjugation in early life earned the right to command it later. . . . Having fitted themselves to others' wishes over an extended period of time, they could bring long-accumulated discipline to bear on business affairs and on those below them in their line of command, including daughters, who would grow up to repeat the cycle.[56]

Although this argument is most rational, it does not explain why the young women were not broken entirely. I would suggest they were not broken because there must have existed enough identification with the active-masculine mother to keep the daughters from complete psychological annihilation.[57]

Questions of affection were probably another matter. Haskell again points the way to some interesting considerations but does not proceed far enough in her inquiry. The "corollary of compensation," which she posits as having been at work in the subjugation of daughter to mother,

> may also have applied to affection. Tenderness toward small children is never mentioned. We do not know the circumstances of Margaret's girlhood, though it is likely that she was sent to live in the household of some suitable woman, after the practice of the time. That these arrangements were frequently miserable is attested by the correspondence concerning them. Margaret's early married years were spent predominantly in the company of her mother-in-law, including such periods as those when Agnes was chastising her daughter Elizabeth. The affection withheld by her and from her elsewhere in life seems to have found compensation in her marriage to John Paston.[58]

What Haskell does not notice here is that it would have been well-nigh impossible for these women to love each other in the nurturing way of mother and daughter. Their affections, as seen in the letters, were directed toward their husbands, that is, exclusively toward men.

The Paston women emerge from their correspondence as having been directive and authoritarian; if they and their daughters supported each other, they would have been acquiescing in a gentleness they seem to despise linked as it has been to passivity. That women like the Pastons were not in the majority is almost completely self-evident: most women have identified with their mothers—or with a mother-surrogate—and most women have been passive, to this day.

We can see the symbolic inculcation of this passivity in one of the plays of the *Ludus Coventriae* cycle of the fifteenth century. What better model for mothers and daughters than Our Lady and Her mother, Anne? In the section called "Mary in the Temple," Joachim and Anne bring the three-year-old child to the high priest in Jerusalem; Mary has been promised as "a servant of God," Joachim relates, and if they "tarry" in delivering her to the Temple, the parents might incur God's wrath; Anne agrees:

> "It is as you say; husband, let us take Mary between us and procede to the Temple.—Daughter, the angel told us you would be a queen. Would you like to go and see that lord who is to be your husband and learn to love him and lead your life with him? Tell your father and me here: let's see what your answer is. Would you like to be a pure maiden, and also God's wife?[59]

Mary replies with—according to Anne—the wisdom of a twenty-year-old:

> "Father and mother, since it would be pleasing to you according to your vow, truely I would like to be God's chaste servant while I am alive; but to be God's wife! I was never worthy. I am the simplest creature ever born in a body and I have heard you say that God should have a sweet mother— that I might live to see her! God grant me for His mercy that I may be able to set my hands under her feet![60]

Joachim approves of this attitude in his daughter, remarking to Anne, "Wife, I am very joyful to see our daughter thus," and she concurs.[61]

Joachim prays, offering up Mary as the servant of God, and Mary takes leave of her parents with a humility never yet seen in a three-year-old child but evidently considered ideal:

> "Now, Our Lord, I thank you that these are my father and mother. Most meekly I beseech you that I may kiss you. Now forgive me if ever I made you angry."[62]

Mary's father assures her that she has offended neither God nor man and hopes that God will keep her that way. Anne, however, bids her to "Think, swete daughter, of your mother Anne—your swimming away smites me to the heart."[63] When Joachim comments that Mary is the model for what all children should be, Anne agrees, but her last request in the scene is a natural one: "Husband," she says, "if it please you, let us not go away from here until Mary is within the Temple—I would not for all the earth see her fall!"[64]

While the entire scene is obviously meant to present a paradigm of proper behavior and also must endow Mary with the degree of saintliness commensurate with her being the Mother of God, Anne is indeed depicted here as a natural mother. She must, of course, be willing to complete the vow and fulfill the promise which she and Joachim have made; she must also, as a model mother of a daughter, present what resembles an arranged marriage to her in the most favorable terms. But we see her grief as Mary goes from her, as the playwright permits us to see that her passivity is not unclouded by having to give up her child.

A work that deals most centrally with the mother-daughter relationship in the medieval period and that, moreover, resolves the problems under discussion within the cultural context of the period is *The Lay of the Ash Tree* by the great Breton writer, Marie de France.[65] This is a poetic work, of course, and not a demographic survey. One does not know how many mother-daughter relationships were resolved in the terms the story suggests symbolically, but it certainly takes into account the major complexities that still beset the mother-daughter bond in a patriarchal society.

The Lay of the Ash Tree tells of one woman who slanders another by claiming that the twins the second woman has given birth to result from her having slept with two husbands, an ancient superstition connected with twin births. The slanderer is punished by fate in that she herself gives birth to twins but, this time, the infants are girls. In a state of terrible anxiety, the mother is prepared to do away with one of the children. As she tells one of her women-in-waiting,

> "The only way to keep me from shame, is that one of my children should die. It is a great sin; but I would rather trust to the mercy of God, than suffer scorn and reproach for the rest of my life."[66]

The women attending her do not back away in horror and revulsion but instead take pity on her, and, sympathetic to her plight and her anxiety, dissuade her from taking measures to have the infant killed:

> The women about her comforted her as best they might in this trouble. They told her frankly that they would not suffer such wrong to be done, since the slaying of a child was not reckoned a jest.[67]

One woman-in-waiting, who loves the lady particularly, suggests an alternative solution:

> The lady had a maiden near her person, whom she had long held and nourished. The damsel was a freeman's daughter, and was greatly loved and cherished of her mistress. When she saw the lady's tears, and heard the bitterness of her complaint, anguish went to her heart like a knife. She stooped over the lady, striving to bring her comfort.
> "Lady," she said, "take it not so to heart. Give over this grief, for all will yet be well. You shall deliver me one of these children, and I will put her so far from you, that you shall never see her again, nor know shame because of her. I will carry her safe and sound to the door of a church. There I will lay her down. Some honest man will find her, and,—please God—will be at the cost of her nourishing.[68]

The infant, wrapped in a special samite cloth clasped by a jewel, is left on the steps of a convent. She is taken in and reared by the abbess. Thus the first part of the tale ends.

What is the significance of this beginning? We are, at long last, in the ladies' chamber, and beside the childbed. Very clearly depicted, in spare symbolic terms, is the relationship of women to childbirth and to the birth of female children in particular within patriarchal society. The archaic nature of the slander—by Marie's time, as the narrative indicates, the dual father theory of twin births was not generally held—sets the ominous tone. Adultery on the part of women was punishable by death, the compassion of Jesus in this matter never overturning the Mosaic code.[69] The slander represents the dangerous rivalry between women who should be at one in their purposes and ends.

The guilt the lady feels at the birth of her own twins is related to her malevolent feelings and destructive conduct in the past. Moreover, the birth of twin girls seems to her to signify a greater punishment. Now her own life is threatened, for, as Emily Coleman suggests, adultery was frequently taken more seriously than infanticide, especially when girl children were concerned.[70] That the women-in-waiting are not particularly shocked by the mother's attitude indicates their understanding of her terror and their identification with it. One such woman, whom the lady has "loved and cherished," makes the suggestion of removing but not killing the child. In other words, it is a young woman with faith in the lady's capacity for motherly love who precipitates the movement towards what will ultimately be the lady's epiphany and redemption.

In the next part, set many years later, a great lord, visiting the convent where Frene, the abandoned daughter, lives, falls in love with the girl and convinces her to run away with him and to become his concubine. He cherishes her but, under pressure from the knights of his kingdom, arranges to marry another. The other, as one would suspect, is the twin sister of Frene.

Although she is to be cast off, Frene loves the lord so much that she finds his wedding bed insufficiently bedecked and, Griselda-like, places her samite swaddling cloth upon it. The lady, mother of the twin girls, recognizes the fabric. At this moment, the mother is forced to confront her own guilt and to recognize her long-lost daughter.

The mother, moreover, exhibits a desire to right wrongs and wishes not only to acknowledge the girl but to succor her. Calling Frene to her, the mother examines the ring that had also been left with the baby:

> The lady looked closely on the ring, when it was brought. She knew her own again, and the crimson samite on the bed. No doubt was in her mind. She knew and was persuaded that Frene was her very child. All words were spoken, and there was nothing more to hide.
> "Thou art my daughter, fair friend."[71]

The sense of enormous release, of there being "nothing more to hide," causes the lady to fall into a swoon, and we are told of "the pity that was hers": in identifying with her daughter—in recognizing her—she can now reconcile the feelings within herself.[72]

She sends for her husband, who rushes to the bedchamber. The lady confesses her guilt to him:

> "Husband, my offense is so black, that you had better give me absolution before I tell you the sin. A long time ago, by reason of lightness and malice, I spoke evil of my neighbor, whenas she bore two sons at a birth. I fell afterwards into the very pit that I had dug. Though I told you that I was delivered of a daughter, the truth is that I had borne two maids. . . . Such a sin will out. The cloth and the ring I have found, and I have recognized our maid, whom I had lost by my own folly."[73]

The power to absolve or resolve is still the husband's, but the mother is now ready to confront that power. She has found the courage she lacked at the birth of her daughters and, now able to face the censure and threat that might come from her husband and from society, she can ask him to forgive her and to accept their child. What has given her this courage? Her own acceptance of her daughter and therefore of herself.

As in Chaucer's "The Franklin's Tale," one brave and loving gesture engenders another; the father of Frene says:

> "Wife, if your sin be double, our joy is manifold. Very tenderly hath God dealt with us, in giving us back our child. I am altogether joyous and content to have two daughters for one. Daughter, come to your father's side."[74]

Thus, all ends happily in *The Lay of the Ash Tree*. Frene marries the knight who "knew such joy as was never yet," the sister is well-married to another lord, and upon Frene's marriage "for dowry her father gave her the half of his heritage."[75] This ending has been made possible, however, only by the mother's departure from the passive role, the role of victim, and her active identification with the maid whom, she says, "I had lost by my own folly."

It is largely, then, a question of images: the mother seeing herself in the daughter, the daughter being reflected in the mirror of her mother.

Whereas some women in the religious literature support their daughters in pursuit of freedom and autonomy,[76] those women who are described as remaining within the patriarchal structure of the family are committed to inculcating passivity in their female offspring. The women who brought their daughters to abbeys or nunneries—in actuality and in literature—in the hope that there the young women would lead better, nobler lives, were they not saying, in effect, that the status of a male, achieved through virginity, was far better than that of a woman, crowned and confirmed in motherhood?

So mothers might teach their daughters to weep and serve and weep again; they might teach them, as does the Wife of Bath's "dame," to snare a man; they might mix love drinks for them, as Iseult's mother does; they might bundle them off to convents or prepare them to lead an anchoress' life of contemplation. What they do not seem to be able to do in the literature, generally speaking, is to give them respect and honor for full-blown biological womanhood. What the daughters must have seen in the mirror of their mothers' lives was that "many, if not most, women believed themselves to have been born inferior, and if they did not subscribe wholeheartedly to the idea, they seldom jeopardized their positions by saying so."[77]

A little document—one can scarcely call it a poem—exists that confirms this opinion. It is in verse, dates from approximately 1430, and is called "How the Good Wife Taught Her Daughter." I am not convinced that its author was a woman, but the work certainly sets forth a lesson plan it seems likely medieval mothers might have followed. It urges obedience and caution and seems to hold staying out of trouble a primary goal, indicating that whatever else might have been withheld in medieval exchanges between mother and daughter, the conviction that life was fraught with danger was not withheld. The best way to avoid trouble was subordination:

> As to that man who will wed you with a ring,
> Love him and honor him most of all earthly things;
> Meekely answer him, and not like an upstart,
> And so you may appease his mood, and be his darling;
> > A fair word and a meek one
> > will slake wrath,
> > > My dear child.

You should be fair of speech, cheerful and mild,
True in word and deed, in conscience good;
Keep yourself from sin, from mischief, from blame,
And look to it that you carry yourself so that
No man can shame you; whoever leads
a good life will win the game,
My dear child.[78]

NOTES

1. From W. B. Yeats, "Among School Children," *Selected Poems and Two Plays of William Butler Yeats*, ed. M. L. Rosenthal, (New York: Collier Books, 1962), p. 117.

2. Robert Briffault, *The Mothers* (New York: Grosset and Dunlop, 1963).

3. *See* Ashley Montague, *The Natural Superiority of Women*, rev. ed. (New York: Collier Books, 1974), p. 58, n. 1.

4. *See* J. J. Bachofen's pioneering work, *Myth, Religion and Mother Right* (Princeton, N.J.: Princeton University Press, 1967). Some feminists still cling to the historical matriarchy theory; *see* Elizabeth Gould Davis, *The First Sex* (New York: Penguin Books, 1973), pp. 19-132.

5. Andrea Dworkin, *Woman Hating* (New York: E.P. Dutton, 1974), p. 115.

6. Henry B. Biller, *Father, Child and Sex Role* (Lexington, Mass.: C. C. Heath & Co., 1971), p. 106; *see* his chapter on "Fathering and Female Personality Development," pp. 103-18.

7. By encouraging a rivalry for protection and love; *see* chapters 5 and 6.

8. As in the attitudes towards women doctors and midwives; *see* C. H. Talbot, "Dame Trot and Her Progeny," *Essays and Studies* 25 (1972): 1-14.

9. *Juliana of Norwich*, ed. Franklin Chambers (London: Gollancz, 1955), p.160.

10. *Legendys of Hooly Wommen*, ed. Mary S. Serjeantson (London: E. E. T. S., 1938), p. 66.

11. Ibid., p. 67.

12. Ibid., p. 67.

13. Dworkin, *Woman Hating*, p. 115.

14. Serjeantson, *Legendys*, p. 67.

15. Ibid., p. 244.

16. Ibid., p. 246.

17. Ibid., p. 247.

18. Ibid., p. 251.

19. As midwives, for example; *see* Thomas R. Forbes, "Perrette the Midwife: A Fifteenth Century Witchcraft Case," JHMAS (1973): 124-9.

20. I refer to the charming literal-mindedness of the Gawain or Pearl-poet's narrators and to Langland's earthy details such as the flea on the miser's threadbare coat in *Piers Plowman*.

21. The accepted view from Philo to Thomas Aquinas and beyond; *see* the summary of Bulough, "Medieval Medical and Scientific Views of Women," *Viator* 4 (1973).

22. J. H. W. Bennett and G. V. Smithers, *Early Middle English Verse and Prose* (Oxford: Clarendon Press, 1966), p. 77.

23. "Woman in the Marginalia of Gothic Manuscripts," in *The Role of Woman in the Middle Ages* (Albany: SUNY Press, 1975), pp. 121ff.

24. Eileen Power, *Medieval Women* (Cambridge: Cambridge University Press, 1975), p. 11.

25. The debate goes on as to whether the fabliaux were composed by students, the gentry, or the new middle class who populate the tales and ape the manners of the court.

26. This tale is originally from France; *see* Bennett and Smithers, *Early Middle English Verse and Prose*, p. 77.

27. Ibid., pp. 91-2.

28. In almost all the tales, the students get the best of the burghers and their wives, as in Chaucer's classic "The Miller's Tale," and many mock the higher clergy.

29. F. N. Robinson, ed., *The Works of Geoffrey Chaucer* (Boston: Houghton-Mifflin, 1957), p. 59:

> "A, false traitour! false clerk!" quod he,
> "Thow shalt be deed, by Goddes dignitee!
> Who dorste be so boold to disparage
> My doghter, that is come of swich lynage?"
> "Thow shalt be deed, by Goddes dignitee!

30. I will be citing the translation of William Mathews from his *Later Medieval English Prose* (New York: Appleton-Century-Crofts, 1963).

31. *See* Eileen Power, *Medieval Women*, pp. 76-80.

32. Matthews, *Later Medieval English Prose*, p. 280.

33. Power, *Medieval Women*, p. 19; Geoffrey's attitude toward punishment discussed.

34. Matthews, *Later Medieval English Prose*, pp. 279-80.

35. Ibid., p. 280.

36. Ibid., pp. 280-1.

37. I cite the translation of W. W. Comfort of Chrétien's *Arthurian Romances* (London: Dent, 1914); this is on p. 8.

38. Ibid., p. 9.

39. Ibid., p. 9.

40. Ibid., p. 19.

41. Chrétien, living at Troyes between 1160 and 1172, was attached to the court of Marie de Champagne, who surrounded herself with other powerful and cultivated women.

42. *See* chapter 5; the adopting mother in this (originally French) romance plays a much greater part in the girl's life than does her natural mother.

43. *See* James H. Gairdner, ed., *The Paston Letters* (New York: AMS Press, 1965).

44. In "The Paston Women on Marriage," *Viator* 4 (1973): 459–71.

45. Ibid., p. 460.

46. Ibid., p. 469.

47. Ibid., p. 470. Italics are mine.

48. Ibid. footnote, p. 470, indicates that she bases her conclusions on the correspondence of one or two families.

49. *See* Gairdner, *Letters* 78, 189, 518, 502, 513. The women ran these estates while their husbands were away in London.

50. Haskell, "The Paston Women," p. 464.

51. Vern L. Bullough, "Medieval Medical and Scientific Views of Women," *Viator* 4 (1973).

52. Power, *Medieval Women*, pp. 43–4.

53. Dworkin, *Woman Hating*, p. 115.

54. Haskell, "The Paston Women," p. 467; Gairdner, *Letters* 607, 617, 479, 601, 607.

55. Letter 71; Elizabeth Paston refused the family choice of husband and was beaten severely over a long period of time.

56. Haskell, "The Paston Women," p. 470.

57. Some of the daughters—Anne, for example—seem to have yielded; *see* ibid., p. 469, and Gairdner, *Letters* 695, 732, 733.

58. Haskell, "The Paston Women," p. 470.

59. I refer to the K. S. Block edition of the *Ludus Coventriae* (London: E.E.T.S., 1960). This is to be found on p. 72.

60. Ibid., p. 72.

61. Ibid., p. 73.

62. Ibid., pp. 73–4.

63. Ibid., p. 74.

64. Ibid., p. 74.

65. All references and quotations from *The Lay of the Ash Tree* are from the translation of Eugene Mason, *Lays of Marie de France and Other French Legends* (London: Dent, 1954).

66. Ibid., p. 93.

67. Ibid., p. 93.

68. Ibid., p. 93.

69. *See* Heath Dillard, "Women in Reconquest Castile," *Women in Medieval Society*, ed. Susan Mosher Stuard (University of Pennsylvania Press, 1976); p. 81, for example: a woman caught *in delicto flagrante* had little recourse to law, Mosaic or other.

70. And infanticide was not exactly unknown; *see* Emily Coleman, "Infanticide in the Early Middle Ages," in *Women in Medieval Society.*

71. Mason, trans., *Lays*, p. 100.

72. Ibid., p. 100.

73. Ibid., pp. 100–01.

74. Ibid., p. 101.

75. Ibid., p. 101.

76. *See* C. Horstmann, ed., *The Lives of Women Saints of Our Countrie of England* (London: E.E.T.S., 1886), pp. 39, 40, 102–03, 54, 59. In these reports of Anglo-Saxon saints, the mothers frequently dream of their daughters becoming nuns and sometimes enter the convents with them.

77. Mary R. Mahl and Helene Koon, *The Female Spectator: English Women Writers Before 1800* (Bloomington, Indiana: Indiana University Press and The Feminist Press, 1977), p. 5.

78. Frederick J. Furnival, ed., *Manners and Meals in Olden Time* (London: E.E.T.S., 1868).

THE FANTASY OF POWER: OLD HAGS AND ANCIENT CRONES

*"Women when they are old enough to
have done with the business of being
women, and can let loose their strength,
must be the most powerful creatures
in the whole world."*
—Isak Dinesen[1]

Although "the weaker sex" has not obtained or exercised great power or authority in the course of Western history, one of the most common accusations of misogynists has been that women wield tremendous power, or would do so if permitted to live with full human rights. As Sarah Pomeroy has pointed out, while Greek women were virtually incarcerated in the houses of Athens, where even female companionship seems to have been distinctly limited, their tragic counterparts strode upon the stages; and Antigone, Electra, and Medea have come to inhabit the imagination of European man as certainly as any "real" female creatures.[2] The attribution of destructive power to women has continued unabated over the centuries in our literature; if Medea was skilled in the preparation of poisons, Mrs. Portnoy does well with a kitchen knife; and a vast number of female characters in between have been depicted—by men— as threatening, castrating, scheming, and possessing almost magical powers.[3] Actual women, while kept in the deepest possible ignorance, unschooled and untaught, were thought to possess a dangerous and forbidden wisdom.[4]

The several possible explanations for this apparent paradox range from the imagined tenacity of the phallic mother to the manifestation of the oppressor's guilt.[5] It is not to my purpose here to explore the complex motivation for this phenomenon in general; I do wish, however, to concentrate on the fear of and hostility toward old women who are represented with their daughters or with other women young enough to be their daughters. The witches, the hags, the crones, and the sorceresses who populate folktale and legend not only symbolize, I believe, the worst fears of men in regard to women but also represent a *female* fantasy:

that of the powerful and sympathetic mother whose amulets and charms give both the young woman and the old some control over the real world.

The figures of mother-in-law and midwife testify to the emotional and symbolic distortion of the relationship of old woman to young one in our civilization. Sigmund Freud, calling attention to the true nature of mother-in-law jokes, stipulates that ridicule, a defense against fear and/or anxiety, is displaced from the mother—the man's mother, toward whom the man would have ambivalent feelings—and redirected towards the mother of the man's wife.[6] Ambivalent feelings may be aggravated by the overt sexuality of marriage, provoking an entire constellation of defenses. Age-old taboos and sanctions functioning in the separation of the affectionate and sexual emotions, now threatened by the resemblance of wife to mother, may be made fast once again by dividing the wife, so to speak, into an object of sexual attraction and an object of revulsion. Whatever is threatening to the male in his oedipal anxiety is then redirected towards the wife's mother. Freud's theory is indirectly corroborated by anthropologists such as Briffault, who discusses the role of the mother of a wife in matriarchal societies. He relates that the woman's mother not infrequently evoked terror in her son-in-law; in one tribe, for example, it was customary for the son-in-law to flee at the very sight of her.[7]

Depictions of mothers-in-law are few in the medieval period, both in the literature and in historical writings, although they do appear in *The Paston Letters*, for example, and in the *fabliaux*. The midwife, however, provides an illustration of the fears and fantasies evoked by an older woman in conjunction with a young one. Helene Deutsch relates that in the labor of childbirth, the midwife becomes the symbolic figure of her mother to the woman.[8] Men were obviously afraid of midwives, who were not only scorned and demoted to the lowest place in society, but accused of witchcraft as well. In his documentation of one such case, that of Perrette the midwife, a contemporary researcher remarks that

> Clearly, there was the temptation for the midwife to practice the black arts. Witchcraft, according to a leading authority, was widespread during this period, and its devotees were to be found everywhere. The midwife, at that time usually an ignorant and incompetent elderly woman, received meagre fees, occupied the lowest level of society, and lived a lonely and probably unhappy life. An opportunity for prestige in the community, power of

sorts, the confidences of her neighbors, additional fees, and the unholy delights of the witches' sabbath evidently drew some of these poor creatures into "the old religion," even at peril of merciless punishment if they were apprehended by the authorities and with the certain expectation, in any case, of eternal damnation.[9]

An interesting combination of insight and misinformation in the passage above shows that, although many prejudices have been dismissed and overcome, the strongest linger. Certainly most midwives were very poor and led marginal lives; but, as recent evidence has shown, although they might have been ignorant of Latin and indeed might have been illiterate, there is no reason to believe that midwives were in general "ignorant and incompetent."[10] On the contrary, the evidence suggests that they were more knowledgeable in the workings of the body than many a medieval doctor trained in the schools.[11]

As we see in the trial of Jacqueline Felicie, in Paris, 1322, practitioners of medicine who had *not* been educated in the physicians' subjects like astrology and the theory of the humours would be more likely to win the approval of modern medicine. Those banned from the schools (women, Jews, and the like) had only empirical evidence, rather than theory, to rely upon. As they might be accused of such errors as actually feeling the bodies and limbs of their patients, their reputations—seeing that they were unlicensed—depended upon their success in healing.[12] Midwives, in contrast to most medieval physicians, at least were acquainted with women's bodies.[13] This was acknowledged by the Parisian court in the verdict on Perrette in 1408. Although she was found to have procured a dead fetus for sorcerer—he pretending, by the way, to be a physician— she was pardoned because of her "great renown and skill at deliveries," an office she "performed and carried out well and dutifully for the space of twenty years and more . . . without arousing any complaint," acquiring "by her loyalty, diligence, and industry . . . the affection and favor of many noble ladies, women of the middle class, and others."[14]

This evidence has not prevented the researcher just quoted from concluding that most midwives were ignorant; and the relative medical wisdom shown by these women did not prevent their prosecution in the Middle Ages either. It is interesting to note in case after case that the charges were brought by men.[15] Indeed, it seems that it was this very

quality of knowledge that men of the medieval period found so threatening. Moreover, what the midwife knew about was the mystery of birth,
the source of women's latent power and men's latent envy.[16] Finally, if
the midwife does represent the woman's mother in the birthing situation
—not the passive mother so often portrayed but one actively and effectively helping her daughter achieve what only a woman can bring to
pass—the contempt for and fear of the midwife and the accusations
leveled against her for witchcraft stem from reactions to the situation in
which the powerful mother-surrogate helps the daughter achieve
exclusively feminine ends.

How do such projections and transferences manifest themselves in the
literature of medieval England? Marianne Moore has written that
while the protagonists in Irish tales might not always have mothers they
all have grandmothers."[17] It might be said of more than a few female
characters that they have surrogate mothers of the Loathely Lady type,
particularly in that part of medieval literature influenced by Celtic lore.

To begin with the most familiar, although not the most explicit,
example, let us consider the Wife of Bath, whose tale is a descendant of
one of the Gawain stories and whose hag's transformation comes from
the Irish, too.[18] In the Irish versions, and in Gower's "Tale of Florent,"
the Loathely Lady figure has herself been the victim of an enchantment,
but the inimicable Chaucer internalizes the notion of enchantment and
turns it to wish-fulfillment instead. The enchantments in "The Wife of
Bath's Prologue and Tale" have to do with the psychology of youth and
age, beauty and sexual attraction. The first mention of enchantment is
not in the fairy tale the Wife relates but in her prologue, when she has led
the pilgrims up to her courting of her fifth husband, Jankyn the clerk.
How does she snare the young and "daungerous" Jankyn?[19] "I assured
him," she relates," that he had enchanted me":

> My dam taught me that subtle trick.
> And also I said I dreamed of him all night,
> That he would have slain me as I lay supine,
> And that my whole bed was full of actual blood.
> And yet I hoped that good would come of it,
> For blood betokens gold, as I was taught.
> And all was false; actually I hadn't dreamed it at all,
> But I always took the advice of my dam,
> In this matter as in other things as well.[20]

The real "enchantment" that the Wife's mother has taught her, then, is how to snare a man in his own guilt and fear (she has also accused him of witchcraft in the passage). Chaucer thus is able to air the medieval male notion that mothers taught their daughters spells and to have the Wife dispel that notion with a wink and a laugh.

Enchantment reappears in the tale itself where the Wife of Bath has projected herself into the character of the old hag or Loathely Lady whose magical powers are such that she can produce—for love—a beautiful young girl and once again win over the man. The Loathely Lady, that is, receiving the fealty of the young knight, becomes again her youthful self—and what is a woman's youthful self but her daughter?

In "The Wife of Bath's Tale" mother and daughter figures are collapsed into one, but in other variations of the adventures of Gawain, the old woman and the young are paired.[21] In some versions, in fact, the old woman is the natural mother of the young girl.

One need not look very far in Irish or Celtic literature for the figure of the old sorceress allied with the young heroine, as in "The Son of the King of Erin."[22] This folktale provides a symbolic illustration of the mother-daughter bond and a symbolic resolution of the threatening oedipal situation as well. The only son of the king of Erin gambles with a giant; they play at last for mortal stakes: for each other's head. The youth loses and makes the standard folktale agreement to meet the giant in a year and a day. At that time, the young man sets out to meet his doom, with grief and lamentations. En route, he comes to the house of three old women. The first of these knows him, welcomes him, attends him with great gentleness and courtesy, and sends him on to her two sisters. The last of the sisters tells the young man how to save his head. He must follow an unwinding ball of thread, which will lead him to the giant's three daughters, one of whom will rescue him. The young man follows the hag's instructions, arrives at the giant's home, and makes an alliance with Yellow Lily, the youngest of the daughters. She helps him in numerous trials, even giving him her body to use as a ladder in one instance. With her aid, the son of the king of Erin returns to the court of his parents and at last takes Yellow Lily as his wife.

The tale obviously concerns the struggle of youth to achieve its own life, take its place in society, and come to terms with its parents and itself. The son of the king is described as "almost a young man," that is, one who is about to come of age, and we are informed that he is "an only son" of whom his parents are "very careful and fond."[23] Thus there is a dramatic intensification of the ordinary adolescent situation. As in many folk and fairy tales, the parental images are divided: the giant is a father-surrogate—the threatening, castrating father—while the king is the "good" father; the old women who aid and abet the young man are mother-surrogates.[24] Renewed oedipal fears at coming of age are symbolized here, but the young man is directed by the mother figures toward a young woman and he is also able to escape the giant-father's jealous wrath.[25]

What does this tale tell us about women and about mothers and daughters in particular? First of all, the image of the all-knowing and all-powerful mother dominates. For the son, there is danger in forbidden contact with her. Each of the old women is equipped with hideous fang-like teeth, which symbolize the *vagina dentata*. The old women, however, do not threaten the giant's daughter, Yellow Lily. This is the difference between most symbolic representations in medieval literature of mother-surrogates and their daughters and the pattern in *Eros and Psyche*, where Venus is the mother-rival or phallic mother, putting obstacles in the way of Psyche's search for Eros.[26] Like Psyche, Yellow Lily risks her life for the son of the king of Erin. The obstacles are set here by her father the giant. The old women are enablers. The sense of continuity from generation to generation of women is symbolized in the ball of yarn that the young man must unwind on his way to salvation. Yellow Lily also helps the young man find, in the first test he undergoes, the "slumber pin" the giant's great-grandmother lost when she was a girl.[27] This detail, too, emphasizes the continuity rather than the disjunction of women's aims.

In "The Son of the King of Erin," both women and men find harmony and peace; the young man returns to his home and all finally accept and celebrate his marriage to Yellow Lily. Young and old women have worked together with singularity of purpose, but for the good of the young man as well. This is not the case in most of the tales of Gawain, where the male characters are frequently threatened by the women's power.

The most skillfully crafted of these tales, in English at least, is the courtly *Sir Gawain and the Green Knight* of the fourteenth-century alliterative revival. Generally emphasized in the criticism of this work are Gawain's intelligent strength and human failing, the playfulness of

Bercilak, and the wily and seductive lady; vivid also are the contrasts of wilderness and court, indoors and outdoors, Gawain's winter journey when the rain freezes in the chinks of his armor, the warmth and gaiety of the respite in Bercilak's castle. Noted but less prominent are such details as the picture of the Virgin painted on the inside of Gawain's shield. An old witch-like woman is present at Bercilak's table; she is linked by the poet—through proximity and direct contrast—with the young and beautiful would-be seductress of Gawain. Bercilak's wife is, of course, the fairest of women; but the second woman is a hideous "auncian," although she is surrounded by attendants.[28] "But these ladies were most dissimilar in appearance, / for if the young one was pretty, the other was just as dried-up."[29] If the cheeks of the young one are "rich red," the cheeks of the old one are "roughly wrinkled"; one wears a head-dress bedecked with pearls that reveals her breast and throat "more beautiful than snowy hillsides," while the old one is covered by a neck-piece that exposes a "black chin."[30] The poet further describes the old woman's physical ugliness, allowing little question of her lack of sexual charms: her brows are black, her lips are devoid of flesh, and bleary. Although she must have been a great lady, she has a short, thick body and broad, bulging buttocks. In brief, the narrator tells us, a man could think of having more pleasure with the lovely one beside her.[31] Thus the poet goes to great lengths to convince the reader of the hideousness of the hag and relates her closely—in a point-by-point comparison—to the young woman.

R. E. L. Masters, in an excellent book on witchcraft, *Eros and Evil*, writes that in the Western European tradition there are two dominant images of the witch: one is that of the ugly old woman, and the other that of the beautiful young enchantress.[32] Of course, the old hag in the passage cited above is none other than the powerful Arthurian sorceress, Morgan, former pupil of Merlin; and the young woman, Bercilak's wife, seems to be more or less a projection or emanation of the old woman. Both women will receive the blame for the entire year-long episode; and, according to the Green Knight himself, Morgan is responsible for the entire plot, shape-shifting, testing, and all:

> "It was the might of Morgan the Fay, who remains
> In my house, and through her well-learned lore
> Of witchcraft, mastered from Merlin—

For she was in love long ago with that vulnerable sage,—
Certainly you knights know about this from home;
> Morgan the goddess
> She turned into:
> She can bring down the proudest
> And tame them to her ends.

She put me on this path to your famous hall
In order to test the pride of it, to see
If the reputation and great renown of the Round Table
Was true; she enchanted me to beguile your wits,
Because she wanted to make Guenevere suffer
And goad her to death with fear of that same ghoul
That spoke like a ghost with his head in his hands
Before the high table. That's the ancient lady
In my house: she is your aunt, Arthur's half-sister,
The Duchess of Tintagel's daughter, the duchess who,
By Uther, mothered Arthur who now rules.
Therefore I entreat you, sir, to come back
> and meet your aunt."[33]

Obviously, the poet has made Morgan conform to the conventional image of the old witch and emphasizes her power over kings and courts, over Bercilak himself, and over the knights. Her presence in the work is sometimes attributed to plot manipulation, but I believe there is more to these lengthy descriptions and tributes than the covering of a narrative creakiness. Later in the work, Gawain enters upon a diatribe against women after his partial defeat at the Green Chapel. This attack on womankind in general has remained obscure. Gawain's anger at one particular lady—Bercilak's wife—does not seem to justify it, nor will citation of Gawain's irrationality at that juncture explain his choice of women, rather than Arthurian inbreeding, as the subject of his diatribe. I think Gawain's passionate misogyny after the blow from the Green Knight can be better understood if his fit of woman-hatred is seen in conjunction with the appearance of the old sorceress and in conjunction with her explicit powers. Gawain does not curse Bercilak at this point because Bercilak—the Green Knight—is perceived by Gawain as himself an agent or perhaps a dupe of Morgan. Indeed, Bercilak is presented as a kind of prankster, innocent of cruel motive or malicious intent. It is in fact by Morgan's machinations that Gawain has been put to the test; and her scheme has used not only the green Knight's fearful appearance and prowess but the young woman's seductive powers as well. What has truly threatened and weakened Gawain is the lure of the young woman with her protective and magical girdle.

While *Sir Gawain and the Green Knight* has as its major theme the question of the individual's integrity in the face of death, a subsidiary theme is the testing of Gawain's manhood, his virility. The mode of the test and the slight punishment Gawain undergoes suggest an initiation rite in one of its primitive forms. The beheading game, so dear to the Celtic storytellers, represents the threat of castration; and the "nirt in þe nekke" that Gawain receives from the Green Knight is therefore a symbolic wound in more ways than one.[34] It is no accident that the episode at the Green Chapel takes place on the day of the Feast of the Circumcision. The token injury Gawain suffers is a mark of his coming of age and is also a reminder of parental and societal powers.[35] Although the threat of castration seems to come directly from Bercilak with his whetted sword and the temptation to break the taboo is directly presented by the young woman, it has really been the old woman's own incestuous grievances against Arthur and his court which have brought this to pass. Morgan the Fay has almost undone Gawain in her affiliation with the young woman, the figure of the daughter-wife. These two-women-in-one have presented the gravest danger to Gawain. That Gawain blames all womankind becomes consistent with the entire series of events at Bercilak's castle and at the Green Chapel. Gawain perceives all women as being at one in their purposes and provocative of the father-figure's punitive ire. He begins by refusing the Green Knight's offer of peace-making with a snarling irony:

> "And commend me to that courteous, charming wife
> Of yours, both to her and to the other one,
> The honorable ladies, that have wantonly
> Beguiled me with their wiles. . . ."[36]

From this point he generalizes, employing the clichés of medieval misogyny:

> "But it is no surprise to be made a fool of
> And be brought to grief by the wiles of women,
> For Adam here on earth was misled by one,
> And Solomon by many, and Samson in the same way—
> Delilah dealing him his fate—and afterwards
> David was blinded by Bathsheba, to his sorrow."[37]

The motives of all these women seem to him the same: the entrapment, the snare, the desire for power, and the eventual "taming" or emasculation:

> "The men were plagued by their tricks: it would be fine
> To love them, but not believe them, if a man could.
> For these men were the best of their time,
> Blessed beyond others who suffered in the same way—
>   And yet they were beguiled
>   By their women;
>   So if I am now ensnared,
>   I think I should be excused."[38]

Morgan's "taming" of Gawain is represented by the poet as positive in the final analysis, for he must learn—after his petulant and childish outburst—that he is vulnerable and open to error. In this light it is possible to see Gawain's misogynistic fulminations as laughable. Gawain does not think them so, of course; and in less philosophical versions of the tale, the authors neglect the ironies implicit in the plot while leaving bare, so to speak, the symbolic construction. *The Green Knight*, a sixteenth-century redaction, meant for "everyday people,"[39] "moves faster than its aristocratic version," its translator notes, its "action is more succinct, and *the basic conflict is more clearly defined. Sir Gawain has to pit his knightly skill against the witchcraft of Agostes, the Green Knight's mother-in-law."*[40]

The redefined conflict is apparent from the beginning. Sir Bredbeddle, the Bercilak-Green Knight figure, "had a wife whom he loved dearly" and who in turn loves Gawain, whom she has never seen.

> Agostes, her mother, was a witch. If any person, a knight or an ordinary man, had been wounded lightly or grievously, or even slain in battle, she could cure him. She told her son-in-law that he should take a journey but with his appearance completely changed.

"You shall go to Arthur's hall," she told him, "for great adventures shall befall you there that no one ever saw before." All these plans were for her daughter's sake. Because her daughter loved Sir Gawain, Agostes wanted to bring him to her castle to meet her.[41]

All of Agostes' machinations—and thus the entire plot—are for the sake of her daughter's desires, her daughter's sexual purposes, wants, and needs:

While the Green Knight went hunting, Sir Gawain stayed in the castle sleeping in his bed. Then the old witch arose early and went to her daughter.

"Don't be afraid," she said, "but the man you have wanted for many a day is in the castle. Now you can have him. Sir Gawain, the courteous knight, is lodging here all night." She brought her daughter to his bed and said, "Gentle knight, awake for the sake of this beautiful lady, who has loved you dearly. Take her in your arms, and no harm will come to you."[42]

The narrator is so concerned with establishing Agostes at the center of the action that he adds—after the meeting of Sir Gawain and the Green Knight has been fixed—that "All this was accomplished by the enchantment of the old witch."[43]

Moreover, in this popular version of the tale, the narrator depicts the women as on one side and the men on the other. In the fourteenth-century courtly poem, Gawain does not exactly embrace Bercilak after the test at the Green Chapel; Bercilak's invitation is gruffly refused. But in the sixteenth-century work, the Green Chapel episode ends most congenially, the two knights—Gawain and Sir Bredbeddle—setting out for Arthur's court together "with light and happy hearts."[44] As in the works of Thomas Malory, there seems to be an intense longing for the outmoded chivalric code with its fellowship of men. *The Green Knight* is crude enough in structure to reveal some of the fears underlying the intense need for that fellowship. The men band together in response to Agostes, the old witch-mother, and in response to her daughter's demands and needs.

Just as a medieval habit of thought made women more physical than men, so mothers seem to have been perceived as having magical powers in the realm of sexuality. In Beroul's *Tristan and Iseult*, Iseult's mother prepares the potion intended for Marc and Iseult that the lovers, or rather those who are about to become lovers, drink by mistake.[45] It is this association of women with carnal knowledge in the literal sense that underlies many misogynistic assumptions and makes the bond between mother and daughter so threatening to the brave men of *The Green Knight*. If, as G. Rattray Taylor suggests in *Sex in History*, the father-identified warrior-type sees the mother as a betrayer in the oedipal situation, there is no cause for wonder if the same anger, fear, and defensiveness he feels toward his mother is projected onto the mother of his wife.[46]

A natural mother, included here because of her magical or supernatural powers, appears in *The Adventures at Tarn Wadling*, a tale in which Gawain is associated with Guenevere, although as her escort and not as her lover.[47] In this curious cautionary work, Guenevere's mother rises out of a bog to warn her daughter of the consequences of lust and other courtly delights. As Gawain conducts Guenevere through a wilderness, the ghostly hag announces herself. Once, she tells Gawain, she was "the fairest of women. . . more beautiful than even Brangwayne, the beauteous maid to Iseult of the White Hands."[48] Now she is the most hideous of creatures:

> The body of the thing was bare. Its only clothing was smoke, its dark bones visible but smeared hideously with clay. It wailed and groaned like a banshee, screeching madly. It hesitated in its movement toward them, then stood fixed like a rock, pained, confused, and staring insanely. . . . A toad gnawed at the side of the specter's throat. Its eyes were hollow pits, glowing like coals. Snakes circled around close by, but to describe this thing any further would tear out my tongue.[49]

Not only is this female death's head surrounded by the creatures associated with witchcraft—the toad and snakes of the quoted passage—but like her earthly counterparts she is being punished for her illicit sexuality. When she was alive, she tells her daughter,

> "My skin had more color than a rose blooming in the rain. My face was soft as a lily, and I laughed easily. Now I am brought down with Lucifer into this tarn and even look like him. Take me for his witness. For all your freshness, I am your mirror of the future and the mirror for every king and emperor as well."[50]

This metamorphosis has taken place because of Guenevere's mother's concupiscence: "This is what happens when you take lovers, indulge your lusts and delights," said the ghost. "These made me a spirit so I belong low in this tarn. . . . Worms in death now work at their revenge, Guenevere."[51]

Although the lesson the ghost has to teach is not limited to the female sex—she is a "mirror" for "every king and emperor as well"—she does caution women in particular and her daughter most of all, Guenevere's adultery being assumed by the narrator and his audience. Gawain himself was notorious for his dalliance, yet the ghost, we note, is suffering horrible punishment for *once* having broken a vow.[52] It is the male fear of female sexuality that has selected the characters and crimes in this tale. Moreover, this ghost has political astuteness and addresses herself to the problem of man's wars.[53] Carnal knowledge—illicit sexual knowledge —is associated here with knowledge of the world and with prophecy, suggesting that the fear of women's wisdom is basically a fear of their sexual knowledge and power.[54] This knowledge is seen as passed down from mother to daughter, or from midwife and witch to daughter-figure, in an exchange between those who share in the mysteries of birth. Even though Guenevere's mother in this homiletic tale warns her daughter against such knowledge—and therefore does not threaten the male *status quo*—the connection of female sexuality with sorcery, witchcraft, and the transmission of knowledge is nonetheless made.

Interestingly enough, it is Guenevere who is charged with saving her mother's soul. Young, beautiful, and in the safekeeping of a man, she is instructed to succor her mother "with a million masses" and to pray for the soul of one who has broken "God's Laws."[55] In other words, the daughter must in some sense disavow the mother and must not in any case be like her, for if she were to live a life similar to her mother's she would displease the Deity so much that she would be cast into hell to suffer the same torments her ghostly parent is suffering.

The Wedding of Sir Gawain and Dame Ragnell, an analogue of the tale the Wife of Bath uses as her *exemplum,* seems a work meant for an audience of women. Women are portrayed sympathetically in it without exception. Perhaps the author wished to appeal to a powerful courtly lady, for he was in dire straits, as the piteous ending reveals.[56] The author's personal predicament alone, however, cannot account for the sympathetic portrayal of women and the deep understanding of true courtliness and civility. Chaucer, too, has the Loathely Lady in the Wife's fantasy teach the unruly knight that if he wishes to be happy with a woman he must voluntarily yield his sovereignty to her. However, because of the complex structure of *The Canterbury Tales* and Chaucer's individual literary inclinations, the Wife of Bath converts the courtly concept of a woman's sovereignty in love into the kind of power-lust that appears in the *fabliaux*. Chaucer has also turned the erring knight into an outright rapist.[57] Sovereignty in love, according to the codes developed in the South of France, had nothing in common with brute force and power and was in fact its antidote.[58] The true courtly lover achieves a way of being in the world based on participation, rather than conquest. As Frederick Goldin puts it:

> The longing for love is more than a sexual instinct: it is the courtly expression of the longing to be a recognized identity, to be part of a society in which one has some significance. . . in the supreme reality of the courtly world, to a life without love *tot es niens*, there is no life, all is vanity, nothing. Because without love one has no presence in the world.[59]

It is just such a high-minded and civilized view of love and of the bonds between men and women that is manifested in *The Wedding of Sir Gawain and Dame Ragnell*. The basic elements of the Loathely Lady tale are present: a knight, under pain of punishment, must solve a riddle—what do women want most?—and can solve the riddle only with the help of the oldest and ugliest woman in the world. Her assistance saves his life, but for this he must marry her. The knight is then asked by the crone—in the marriage bed and on the marriage night—whether he would rather have her beautiful by day, when he would not be shamed in society by her ugliness, or by night, in which case he would enjoy making love to her. The knight leaves the decision to the hag, who instantly rewards him by transforming herself into a beautiful young woman, to remain that both by day and by night. In the version of the tale now under consideration, the poet emphasizes the graciousness and reciprocity of Dame Ragnell's metamorphosis. *Because* Sir Gawain yields to her and *because* he is truly gracious and courtly in the most noble sense of the word, her transformation becomes possible.

If Dame Ragnell is not the oldest woman in the world in this version, the poet here outdoes even Gower in the description of her ugliness:

> Her face was red, her nose snotted, her mouth wide, her teeth yellow, her eye rheumy, her teeth hung over her lips, and her cheeks were as fat as a woman's hips. Her neck was long and thick, her hair clotted and snarled. Her shoulders were a yard broad, and her breasts were a load for a strong horse. She was formed like a barrel. No tongue can adequately describe how foul she was, but she was ugly enough, and Arthur was dumb-founded.[60]

Although the courtiers are aghast at her ugliness—rather than impressed by her kindness or her wit—Gawain steels himself to fulfill the duties of the marriage bed, the knight in most versions being unwilling or unable to do this. Dame Ragnell is touched: " 'God have mercy,' Dame Ragnell exclaims to him, 'for your sake I wish I were a beautiful woman, for you have such good will.' "[61] It is thus her wish to please him, because he has integrity, that brings about her transformation on their wedding night. She asks him to give her a kiss:

> "I will do more than kiss you," Gawain said, "and before God." He turned toward her and saw beside him the most beautiful woman he had ever imagined with no exceptions.
> "Now, what is your will?" she said quietly.[62]

Gawain, given the choice of having her beautiful by day or by night, responds as a true lover:

> ". . . do as you wish, my lady dear. The choice I put in your hands. Do with me as you wish, for I am bound to you. I give the choice to you. Both my body and my goods, my heart and all parts of me are all yours, to buy and sell—that I swear to God."[63]

So Dame Ragnell is released from her enchantment:

> "Many thanks, courteous knight," said the lady. "Of all the knights in the world you must be the most blessed, for now you honor me. You shall have me beautiful both day and night, and I will be fair and attractive as

long as I live. Therefore do not worry, for my stepmother transformed me by an enchantment, may God have mercy on her. I would have been transformed until the best man in England married me and gave me sovereignty over his body and his goods. I was deformed until that happened. And you, sir knight, courteous Gawain, have given me sovereignty, certainly. . . . Be happy and enjoy yourself, for it has turned out well for both of us."[64]

What the author has emphasized here and throughout in his selection of details and turns of plot is the wish and will of Dame Ragnell to shape the course of her life: to save, to reward, to choose both her husband —"the best man in England" for his courtesy—and the self she would like to be. If this is a wish-fulfillment fantasy, it is one of the highest order. "What all women want" in this tale is the power to love and —released from an enchantment by the courtesy of men—to transform themselves into their most beautiful and perfect forms, their ideals, their daughters.[65] If Dame Ragnell has suffered from the ill-will of a stepmother, she herself, with Gawain's help, can bring forth another self. The author has gone far beyond convention here and has portrayed most philosophically the bond between the beautiful and the ugly, the maiden and the crone.

The centrality of the old woman's saving the man—and producing a new self in the process—in these tales is itself indicative that the hag in these stories is a mother figure.[66] Small wonder, then, if in works concerned with courtly love and gentillesse—works which G. Rattray Taylor would suggest are of a *matrist* persuasion[67]— where the uncivilized knight becomes the suppliant son,[68] the Loathely Lady plot shows up again and again. John Gower, too, employs the story in the *Confessio Amantis*, in "The Tale of Florent." Most interesting in Gower's version is his making the woman who threatens to punish the knight an old woman also: the forbidding mother and the saving mother are juxtaposed.[69] In terms of the oedipal situation, the mother may be seen either as a kind of savior, in which case the father may be seen as an "interloper," or as a "betrayer," in which case there is a generalized hostility towards women and fears of conspiracy between old and young women, mothers and daughters.[70] Gower's presentation of the old, threatening "grantdame" whose evil intentions are overcome by the Loathely Lady indicates a resolution of a conflict in feeling towards the mother— a resolution, one might add, to the good and in a direction away from misogyny. But just as the Loathely Lady character appears with frequency in the medieval period, another female character is also much in evidence, a female character often perceived as just such a "betrayer" of men as the Freudian extreme would indicate.

This character—one of whose literary descendants is of course, the Wife of Bath[71]—is La Vieille, the Old Woman, of *The Romance of the Rose,* Part II, by the twelfth-century French philosopher, scientific popularizer, and misogynist Jean de Meun. It would be absurd to attempt a summary of the attitudes and ideas involved in Jean's encyclopedic work or to attempt an analysis of the relation of Part II to Part I of *The Romance of the Rose.* Part I, written by Guillaume de Lorris some fifty years earlier as strictly an allegory of courtly love, seems at first an odd vehicle for the anticourtly and more broadly philosophical Jean de Meun. The choice of such a vehicle finally lets him refute the courtly notions of Guillaume, or at least to satirize the premises and suppositions of those who would turn the courtly code into a kind of religion. The ennobling of women, or the making of the loved woman into a mother figure, was a contribution of the courtly poets.[72] While La Vieille is indeed a mother figure, she is presented as the kind of mother who, in great guile and shamelessness, furthers the sexual ends of young women and is therefore, with her sexual knowingness, an enemy and a threat to men.

Moreover, if Jean's anticourtly bias and tendency towards misogyny were both temperamentally induced and culturally fostered, he was able to resolve a philosophical paradox with the aid of that bias and tendency. I do not mean to reduce the philosophy of Jean de Meun to a mere prejudice nor do I mean to deny the greatness of his work. I simply wish to point to this previously ignored aspect of it. The paradox in question pertains to the so-called Doctrine of Plenitude, a doctrine that arose from the work of the naturalistically inclined thinkers of the University of Paris and the school of Chartres, whose ideas influenced Jean and who were preoccupied with the scientific problem of creation within the context of Christianity.[73] These philosophers and scientists, men such as Bernard Sylvestre and Alain de Lille, affirmed the greatness and goodness of Nature; Jean elaborates, and stresses the part played by humankind in the work of nature, which was considered, of course, to be the work of God.[74] The problem that arises is the problem of evil within the natural world; both Bernard and Alain thrust this problem to one side: it is a question for theology and theologians, not for natural scientists. Jean de Meun, however, decidedly a moralist as well, was not content to ignore the problem of evil in the natural order as his predecessors had done. The corruption of Nature's ends by women was a readily available if not altogether satisfactory explanation for the fallen state of the world. Following Alain, Jean emphasizes that, alone of all the creation, man errs; and he errs, Jean adds, in good part because of the subversive power of women.

The centuries-old charge against Eve is obvious. Jean, however, unlike many Christian misogynists, does not denigrate sexuality.[75] On the contrary, fecundity and the organs necessary to it, particularly the male genitalia, are highly regarded and praised, as are male attempts at generation such as alchemy.[76] Much of Jean's venom is directed towards La Vieille, the Old Woman, whom he exposes as subversive of all the positive values in sex and generation. Furthermore, while the Old Woman has no supernatural powers, Jean's attack on her exhibits many characteristics of the accusations against witches, although the forms he perceives her subversion taking are not the same.

In a modern English translation, La Vieille has been translated as "the Duenna," which provides some notion of her custodial function. We come to know her through a long confession, and it might be well here to review the context of that monologue. The Lover in Part II, like the Lover of the first part, pursues the Rose, the lovely maiden. Various allegorical aspects of the courting situation appear, i.e., Jealousy, False Seeming, Fair Welcome, and the like; and in both poems, the Lover achieves the Rose. As previously stated, however, Guillaume's work is an allegory of courtly love, in which the presiding God of Love is clearly related to Eros. Jean, using the same allegorical framework, has Nature, Genius, and Reason presiding; the art of love is seen as illusion and treachery, the seduction and betrayal of men by wily women. For Jean, the Rose at the end of the work must be impregnated; consummation of passion without regard to the act of generation seems to him not only not enough, but a kind of perversion.[77]

The Lover is still far from his desired end when the Duenna enters, while the full philosophical nature of the work is not yet clear. There is little doubt, however, as to how to view the old woman. She is, in her own way, formidable; the Lover relates: "No fear felt I of further handicap / If the old hag her convoy to me gave," and Fair Welcome is very nervous indeed:[78]

> Fair Welcome did not dare to make complaint
> Or tell the whys and wherefores of his mood;
> For he knew not if she spoke true or lied.
> Thus insecure, he disavowed his thoughts;
> His heart warned him to put no trust in her.
> Trembling and fearful, he dared heave no sigh,
> So much he'd always feared the vile old crone.
> He wished to guard himself from treachery,
> Which he much feared, . . .[79]

The gullible Fair Welcome, another male dupe, is of course an aspect of the Rose herself. Now the Duenna is to be feared not only because she has experienced much and has much carnal knowledge but also because she is an insidious and ingratiating counselor, more than willing to pass on all she knows to the maiden and to instruct the young girl in the art of love.

> "I was a fair, young, silly fool; and had
> No training in the school of love, where's taught
> The theory. The practice well I knew;
> Throughout my life I've had experience
> That's made me wise, so now I know the game
> Up to the final bout. It were not right
> That I should fail to teach you what I know,
> Since I have had so much experiment.
> He who to young folk counsel gives does well."[80]

Her teaching is presented as an inversion of true wisdom; "You're still unfledged," she tells Fair Welcome, "While I have graduated in my course / And know the science to the very end; / I could uphold a lectureship on love. / The lore of age should not be shunned or scorned."[81] Moreover, this perversion of wisdom is to be used to guide the Rose toward distorted ends, one of which is vengeance upon men. La Vieille has been wronged in her time and in her tutelage seeks to compensate for the wrongs she has undergone:

"Thus I complain; and is there one but you,
Whom I so dearly love, to hear my plaint?
How otherwise can I revenge myself
Except by teaching you my principles?
Fair son, my tutelage is to this end:
That, when you shall be learned, you shall take
Vengeance for me upon the whoremongers;"[82]

The old woman, then, past the age of sexual desirability and using the young, naive maiden to avenge old wrongs, in witch-like fashion urges the girl to commit evil deeds (*maleficium*), advising her also to be mercenary and vain, to flatter and flirt, for the sake of gaining power and control; the Duenna does this not without a certain relish in the very commitment to wrongdoing and deception. In telling Fair Welcome how "women gain men's love," she reveals that the means are numerous traps, lies, and illusions:

"If it should chance a woman is not fair,
She should make up her lacks with dainty dress—
Its elegance offsets her ugliness."

"If she is pale and finds this cause of grief,
Moist unguents in her chamber in a box
She should provide, and always by herself,
In secret, can her color be renewed. "[83]

Every physical flaw must be disguised. If her hands are "rough and calloused," the woman will take care to wear gloves.[84] If her teeth are rotten, she will be sure to smile with closed lips.[85]

The Duenna goes on to enumerate various behavioral deceptions women practice:

"A man should never be too much disturbed
Though women's tears he sees fall thick as rain;
For ne'er she rains such tears or shows such grief
Or such chagrin, except for trickery.
Naught but a ruse the tears of women are;
'Tis not with grief that they are most concerned,
But with the thought how they can best conceal,
By what they say or do, what's in their minds."[86]

Even her charity is pretense that should be used to gain power over men; when a young woman goes about in town, she must take care, the Duenna advises, "Not to forget the alms purse all should see, / She frequently in both her hands will seize / Her cloak, and, stretching wide her arms, stand still."[87]

Description and prescription of female shape-shifting continue for hundreds of lines, and culminate in the following extended simile:

> With care should women always imitate
> The wolf when she desires to steal a sheep.
> That she may fail not, and be sure of one,
> A thousand she assails; she never knows,
> Before she has him caught, which one she'll get.
> A woman everywhere should spread her nets
> To capture all the men, . . .[88]

Here women are predatory and all-devouring, indiscriminate in the pursuit of their ends; entangling, ensnaring. One generation passes on its evil knowledge to the next, and the gullible male is seduced by the wicked collusion of women.

Although Jean de Meun consciously disavowed the existence of the night-witch, and regarded such imaginings as "a specialty of foolish old women," his portrait of the old woman manifests certain psychological resemblances to the commonly held idea of the witch, especially in the popular, rather than the ecclesiastical, imagination.[89] Norman Cohn writes:

> At least in Europe, the image of the witch as a woman, and especially an elderly woman, is age-old, indeed archetypal.
>
> For centuries before the great witch-hunt the popular imagination, in many parts of Europe, had been familiar with women who could bring down misfortune by a glance or a curse. It was popular imagination that saw the witch as an old woman who was the enemy of new life, who killed the young, caused impotence in men and sterility in women, blasted the crops.[90]

The witch was committed to bringing about evil. She was associated both with cannibalism—and here one recalls Jean's image of the wolf devouring the sheep—and with conspiracy. The Duenna's tone is conspiratorial throughout.

In Jean's portrait of the Duenna and in the attack on her counseling of the Rose, the overwhelming impression is one of male vulnerability, something of which Cohn does not write, since his concerns are more political.[91] Masters, however, in *Eros and Evil* is explicit about this matter. The "typical witch who has come down to us is old and ugly and often deformed," he explains, noting that

> in a bow to probability, the beautiful witch tempts men to lust while the crone is more likely to be an enemy of procreation, interfering with potency and conception, and murdering infants. Both witches are sex symbols —foes of marriage and friends of fornication.[92]

The sense of male sexual, emotional, and intellectual inadequacy—i.e., man as dupe—that emerges in the Duenna's lecture resembles that given in witchcraft accusations against women. To these fears Masters links the "physiology of the male, with its tumescence-detumescence mechanism" that "has endowed man with a permanent sense of sexual inferiority."[93]

What Masters does not recognize in the two images of the witch he presents is the mother-daughter model inherent in the pairing. The old crone in *The Romance of the Rose* is dangerous because she passes on her knowledge to the next generation of women—not only her knowledge but also her resentments, grievances, and wrongs. If women's vengeance is feared, the strength of those fears indicates some actual male culpability: slave-owners, too, have been known to fear conspiracy and reprisal from the people they have oppressed. A brief episode, casually related, in one of the Gawain stories may serve as an illustration. The gallant Gawain, a father, a brother, and a lover join forces to destroy the helpless and trusting maiden with whom Gawain has made love. The brother meets his sister:

> "Fie on you, sinful harlot. It is a pity you live so long. I will deal you some hard stripes." He beat her both back and side, then left her and went back to his father.
>
> "Son, I have been worried about you," said his father. "I thought you might be shamed."
>
> "I have beaten my sister," Brandles said, "and I made the knight swear that when we meet again, we will fight until our strength is gone and one of us is slain."

All four of them went home together each helping the other as best he could. The lady went her way wandering far and wide, and they never saw her again.[94]

If men feared the vengeance of women, we need not wonder greatly about the cause.

But what of the women who listened to these tales, or who constituted at least part of the audience for *The Romance of the Rose* or *The Green Knight*? One, Christine de Pisan, that remarkable French woman of letters, took issue with the portraits of women in the *Romance* and indeed wrote a furious literary epistle to refute the ideas of Jean de Meun. I suspect, however, that many women must have reacted in the way Chaucer depicts the Wife of Bath reacting. We find some women susceptible in the medieval period, and later, to suggestions that there were actual old women who could perform magical acts.[95] If male abhorrence grew out of subconscious fears of reprisal from women young and old, the depiction of old women with great powers particularly threatening to men and to patriarchal marriage might not have been displeasing to female readers or listeners. Given the powerlessness of women in general, even when they were queens, the satanic knowledge of the witch, the prophetic insights of the hag, and the shrewd calculations of the lascivious go-between might have constituted an acceptable alternative image, a fantasy of the power that few, if any, natural mothers of actual daughters ever had.

NOTES

1. From the short story by Isak Dinesen, "The Monkey," in *Seven Gothic Tales* (New York: Random House, 1934), p. 119.

2. *See* Sarah Pomeroy, *Goddesses, Whores, Wives and Slaves: Women in Antiquity* (New York: Schocken Books, 1975).

3. Mrs. Portnoy, of Phillip Roth's *Portnoy's Complaint*, follows in an established tradition chronicled by Kate Millett; *see Sexual Politics* (Garden City: Doubleday and Company, 1970) for a history of literary antifeminism.

4. A summary of medieval attitudes towards the education of women appears in Eileen Power's *Medieval Women*, ed. M. M. Postan (Cambridge: Cambridge University Press, 1975).

5. Pomeroy contends that the mother, so obscured in classical Greek culture, loomed large in the collective unconscious of those who tried to deny her. And

see G. Rattray Taylor, *Sex in History* (New York: Harper and Row, 1970), pp. 72–86, for his theory of matrist or patrist repressions.

6. *See* the edition translated by James Strachey under the title *Jokes and Their Relation to the Unconscious* (New York: W. W. Norton, 1963); *see also Totem and Taboo* in *The Basic Writings of Sigmund Freud* (New York: Modern Library, 1938), p. 817ff.

7. *See* Robert Briffault, *The Mothers* (New York: Macmillan, 1931).

8. Helene Deutsch, *The Psychology of Women: Motherhood* (1944 paperback ed., New York: Bantam, 1973), p. 217.

9. Thomas R. Forbes, "Perrette the Midwife: A Fifteenth Century Witchcraft Case," *Journal of the History of Medicine and Allied Science* (1973): 124–9; 124.

10. Barbara Ehrenreich and Deirdre English, *Witches, Midwives, and Nurses: A History of Women Healers* (Old Westbury, N.Y.: The Feminist Press, 1973), p. 3.

11. Ibid., pp. 16–17.

12. C. H. Talbot presents the trial in "Dame Trot and Her Progeny," *Essays and Studies* 25 (1972): 1–14.

13. Vern L. Bullough, "Medieval Medical and Scientific Views of Women," *Viator* 4 (1973): 485–501; on 501: some physicians disapproved of examining women at all!

14. Forbes, "Perrette the Midwife," p. 125.

15. *See* Talbot, "Dame Trot and Her Progeny," pp. 4–6.

16. Womb envy has been paid more and more attention recently; *see,* among other writers, Bruno Bettelheim, *Symbolic Wounds* (New York: Collier Books, 1971); Ehrenreich and English, *Witches, Midwives, and Nurses,* pp. 3–20; Ashley Montague, *The Natural Superiority of Women,* rev. ed. (New York: Collier Books, 1968), pp. 11–55; and Phyllis Chesler, *About Men* (New York: Simon and Schuster, 1978).

17. From "Spenser's Ireland."

18. F. N. Robinson, ed., *The Works of Geoffrey Chaucer* (Boston: Houghton-Mifflin, 1957), pp. 702–3.

19. Ibid., p. 81, ll. 514–5: "daungerous" meaning "hard to please" in this context.

20. Ibid., p. 81, ll. 575–85:

> I bar hym on honde he hadde enchanted me,—
> My dame taughte me that soutiltee.
> And eek I seyde I mette of hym al nyght,
> He wolde han slayn me as I lay upright,
> And al my bed was ful of verray blood;
> But yet I hope that he shal do me good,

For blood bitokeneth gold, as me was taught.
And al was fals; I dremed of it right naught,
But as I folwed ay my dames loore,
As wel of this as of othere thynges moore.

21. As in the sixteenth century *The Green Knight*, Louis B. Hall, ed. and trans., *The Knightly Tales of Sir Gawain* (Chicago: Nelson-Hall, 1976).

22. "The Son of the King of Erin" appears in *Myths and Folktales of Ireland*, ed. Jeremiah Curtin (New York: Dover Books, 1975).

23. Ibid., p. 1.

24. *See* Bruno Bettelheim, *The Uses of Enchantment* (New York: Vintage, 1977), for explication of these common fairy-tale phenomena.

25. In that he does not "covet" the mother but transfers his affections to another object.

26. *See* Erich Neumann's classic Jungian interpretation of *Amor and Psyche: The Psychic Development of the Feminine* (New York and Evanston: Harper and Row, 1962).

27. Curtin, *Myths and Folktales*, p. 8 and p. 243.

28. I refer to the edition of *Sir Gawain and the Green Knight* (CGK) by J. R. R. Tolkien and E. V. Gordon, revised by Norman Davies (Oxford: Clarendon Press, 1967), and will quote from it; see p. 26, 11. 942–3 and 11. 948–9.

29. *GGK*, p. 27, 11. 950–1: "Bot vnlyke on to loke þo ladyes were, / For if þe ȝonge watz ȝep, ȝolȝe watz þat oþer."

30. *GGK*, p. 27, 11. 952–8:

Riche red on þat on rayled ayquere,
Rugh ronkled chekes þat oþer on rolled;
Kerchofes of þat on, wyth mony cler perlez,
Hir brest and hir bryȝt þrote bare displayed,
Schon schyrer þen snawe þat schedez on hillez;
þat oþer wyth a gorger watz gered ouer þe swyre,
Chymbled ouer hir blake chyn with chalkquyte vayles, . . .

31. *GGK*, p. 27, 11. 959–69:

Hir frount folden in sylk, enfoubled ayquere,
Toreted and trelated with tryflez aboute,
þat noȝt watȝ bare of þat burde bot þe blake broȝes,
þe tweyne yȝen and þe nase, þe naked lyppez,
And þose were soure to se and sellyly blered;
A mensk lady on molde mon may hir calle,
                    for Gode!

> Hir body watz schort and þik,
> Hir buttockez balȝ and brode,
> More lykkerwys on to lyk
> Watz þat scho hade on lode.

32. Subtitled *The Sexual Psychopathology of Witchcraft* (New York: Penguin, 1974), p. 169.

33. *GGK*, pp. 67–8, ll. 2446–67:

> "þurȝ myȝt of Morgne la Faye, þat in my hous lenges,
> And koyntyse of clergye, bi craftes wel lerned,
> þe maystres of Merlyn mony hatz taken—
> For ho hatz dalt drwry ful dere sumtyme
> With þat conable klerk, þat knowes all your knyȝtes
>   at hame;
>   Morgne þe goddes
>   þerfore hit is her name:
>   Weldez non so hyȝe hawtesse
>   þat ho ne con make ful tame—
>
> Ho wayned me vpon þis wyse to your wynne halle
> For to assay þe surquidre, ȝif hit soth were
> þat rennes of þe grete renoun of þe Rounde Table;
> Ho wayned me þis wonder your wyttez to reue,
> For to haf greued Gaynour and gart hir to dyȝe
> With glopnyng of þat ilke gome þat gostlych speked
> With his hede in his honde bifore þe hyȝe table.
> þat is ho þat is at home, þe auncian lady;
> Ho is euen þyn aunt, Arþurez half-suster.
> þe duches doȝter of Tyntagelle, þat dere Vter after
> Hade Arþer vpon, þat aþel is nowþe.
> þerfore I eþe þe, haþel, to com to þyn aunt."

34. On the symbolic significance of Gawain's "nirt in þe nekke," *see* Bettelheim, *Symbolic Wounds*.

35. *See* Elizabeth Brewer, ed. and trans., *From Cuchulain to Gawain* (Cambridge: D. S. Brewer, 1973), pp. 1–2: in the Old French *Tale of Carados*, for example, the Green Knight is presented as the *father* of Carados.

36. *GGK*, p. 66, ll. 2411–13:

> "And comaundez me to þat cortays, your comlych fere,
> Boþe þat on and þat oþer, myn honoured ladyez,
> þat þus hor knyȝt wyth hor kest han koyntly bigyled."

37. *GGK*, p. 66, 11. 2414–19:

> "Bot hit is no ferly þaȝ a fole madde,
> And þurȝ wyles of wymmen be wonen to sorȝe,
> For so watz Adam in erde with one bygyled,
> And Salamon with fele sere, and Samson eftsonez—
> Dalyda dalt hym hys wyrde—and Dauyth þerafter
> Watz blended with Barsabe, þat much bale þoled."

38. *GGK*, p. 67, 11. 2420–8:

> "Now þese were wrathed wyth her wyles, hit were a wynne
>   huge
> To luf hom wel, and leue hem not, a leuede þat couþe.
> For þes wer forne þe freest, þat folȝed alle þe sele
> Exellently of alle þyse oþer, vnder heuenryche
>   þat mused;
>   And alle þay were biwyled
>   Wyth wymmen þat þay vsed.
>   þaȝ I be now bigyled,
>   Me þink me burde excused."

39. *See* Louis B. Hall, ed. and trans., *The Knightly Tales of Sir Gawain* (Chicago: Nelson-Hall, 1976), pp. 35–6. All quotations of the tale are from the Hall translation.

40. Ibid., p. 36.

41. Ibid., p. 40.

42. Ibid., pp. 45–6.

43. Ibid., p. 43.

44. Ibid., p. 48.

45. *See* Chapter V; also, Agostes in *The Green Knight* is skilled at preparing potions and salves (Ibid., p. 40).

46. *See* Taylor, *Sex in History*, pp. 72–86 and especially pp. 78–79.

47. A tale of the fifteenth century; *see* Hall, *The Knightly Tales*, pp. 51–5; also R. J. Gates, ed., *The Awntyrs of Arthure at the Terne Wathelyne* (Philadelphia: University of Pennsylvania Press, 1969).

48. All citations refer to the Hall translation; this is on p. 60.

49. Hall, *The Knightly Tales*, pp. 59–60.

50. Ibid., pp. 60–1.

51. Ibid., p. 62.

52. Ibid.

53. *See* Norman Cohn, *Europe's Inner Demons* (New York: Basic Books, 1975), pp. 258–63.

54. *See* R.E.L. Masters, *Eros and Evil* (Baltimore: Penguin, 1974), pp. 169–70; also, Ehrenreich and English, *Witches, Midwives, and Nurses*, pp. 10–15.

55. Hall, *The Knightly Tales*, p. 62.

56. Ibid., p. 175: "Pity him who wrote this story. Jesus, as Thou was born of a virgin, help him out of his sorrows for he is in the hands of many jailers who keep him securely with torture wrong and awful."

57. *Works of Chaucer*, pp. 82ff.

58. *See* Taylor, *Sex in History*, pp. 87–107; also, Maurice Valency, *In Praise of Love* (New York: Farrar, Straus and Giroux, 1975), pp. 38–58. Just how much the new ideals changed actual behavior is still debatable.

59. Frederick Goldin, trans., *Lyrics of the Troubadours and Trouveres* (Garden City, N.Y.: Anchor Press, 1973), p. 11.

60. Citations are to the Hall translation, pp. 159–75; this on pp. 163–4. *See also* B. J. Whiting, ed., "The Weddynge of Sir Gawain and Dame Ragnell" in *Sources and Analogues of Chaucer's Canterbury Tales*, ed. W. F. Bryan and Germaine Dempster (New York: Humanities Press, 1958), pp. 242–67.

61. Hall, *The Knightly Tales*, p. 169.

62. Ibid., p. 171.

63. Ibid., p. 172.

64. Ibid., pp. 172–3.

65. Deutsch, *The Psychology of Women*, p. 217.

66. Ibid.

67. Mother-oriented or identified; see Taylor, *Sex in History*, pp. 72–108.

68. Ibid., p. 94: "under the influence of the new conception of behaviour developed by the troubadours, in which bravery was combined with gentleness and courtesy to women" the "desire for women's approval became the motive for valour." Also, *see* Valency, *In Praise of Love* (New York: Farrar, Strauss, and Giroux, 1975), p. 32: "the romantic lover applies for love in the role of the son and, unconsciously identifying the beloved with the mother, he is fearful and humble and asks for pity."

69. *Confessio Amantis*, ed. Russell A. Peck (New York: Holt, Rinehart and Winston, 1968), pp. 58–71; *see* pp. 59–60 and p. 65 in particular.

70. *See* Taylor, *Sex in History*, pp. 77–8.

71. Chaucer had even translated part of *The Romance of the Rose*.

72. *See* note 68.

73. *See* Brian Stock, *The Cosmology of Bernard Sylvestre* (Princeton: Princeton University Press, 1972).

74. Nature in *The Romance of the Rose* is also a mother figure; it is interesting to note that Jean creates and characterizes the "good mother" only as an abstract universal force whereas La Vieille—although a character in an allegory—is much more naturalistically described.

75. *See* Taylor, *Sex in History*, pp. 51–71, "Medieval Sexual Ideal."

76. And alchemy, a male province, is praised by Jean de Meun for, it seems, this reason.

77. Here Jean follows Alain directly; Alain's cosmogony opens with Nature bemoaning sexual perversion in man.

78. All quotations are from the translation of Harry W. Robbins, ed. Charles W. Dunn (New York: Dutton and Co., 1962); this is on p. 258.

79. Ibid., p. 258.

80. Ibid., p. 265.

81. Ibid., pp. 265–6.

82. Ibid., p. 267, 11. 89–95.

83. Ibid., p. 177, 11. 1–3 and p. 178, 11. 22–5.

84. Ibid., p. 178, 11. 38–9.

85. Ibid., p. 179, 11. 62–70.

86. Ibid., p. 179, 11. 78–85.

87. Ibid., p. 283, 11. 223–5.

88. Ibid., p. 283, 11. 238–44.

89. Cohn, *Europe's Inner Demons*, p. 214.

90. Ibid., p. 251.

91. This is a substantial part of Cohn's thesis; the witches' "Sabbat" is crucial. His conspiracy theory, however, is primarily of political import.

92. Masters, *Eros and Evil*, p. 169.

93. Ibid., p. 170; *see also* H. R. Hays, *The Dangerous Sex* (New York: G. P. Putnam's Sons, 1964).

94. This is from *An Adventure of Sir Gawain*, a popular version of a French tale; *see* Hall, *The Knightly Tales*, pp. 111–25 and p. 125 in particular. Also, *see* Taylor, *Sex in History*, pp. 23–4.

95. Cohn, *Europe's Inner Demons*, p. 210.

FOSTERMOTHERS: WOMEN MOTHERING WOMEN

*"Women's communal bondings. . . can
have the same force, loyalty and
honor as the fellowships traditionally
esteemed among men." —Francine du Plessix Gray*

*"Call on God, my dear. She will help you."
—Mrs. O. H. P. Belmont*[1]

Earlier in this century, Virginia Woolf wrote of the need for literary exploration of the exclusively "feminine" world.[2] Recently, Nina Auerbach in *Communities of Women: An Idea in Fiction* presented a "two millenia old tradition which saw friendship between members of the same sex as more of a cornerstone of human happiness than any 'natural' heterosexual bonding."[3] Auerbach claims that there has been more representation of fellowship among women in literature than is commonly thought.

The words "fellowship" and "friendship" in the context of medieval literature initially bring with them visions of jousting knights or small bands of warriors disembarking on desolate northern coasts. The comitatus of the Anglo-Saxons and the all-male loyalties of chivalry loom large in literary memory. The wailing of women in *Beowulf* one remembers as a response to male deeds; the ladies-in-waiting of the romances seem little but pastel decorations. If the notion of fraternity includes and "embraces notions of honor, dignity and loyalty,"[4] friendship between women in literature—with reference to the medieval period especially—seems an empty concept.

But if one were to bring the clusters of ladies from the periphery of vision into the center, would one find "force, loyalty, and honor" depicted there? These terms must be qualified before they begin to be meaningful in regard to women in medieval literature and in medieval life. "Force, loyalty, and honor" do appear in relationships among and between medieval women; but the force is frequently that of secrecy, the loyalty generic rather than personal, and the honor of the kind that prevents prisoners from betraying each other to the authorities. These relationships cannot be seen in terms of sorority; sisterhood, a variant of mothering, implies equality between or among women. Perhaps because of the threatening conditions and the difficult straits women found themselves to be in during the Middle Ages, many relationships depicted or suggested in the literature exhibit the qualities of protectiveness, solace, consolation, and succor. One woman takes care of another. Perhaps while free and autonomous adults take sisterhood as their model of friendship, the oppressed and endangered need to find mothers in their friends and will in turn act as mothers themselves.

Often, religious figures—from the heads of convents to the Virgin Mary herself—appear as mother-surrogates. Their powers, as one might have expected, are limited: even the Virgin is the mother of a son whom she —his creator—worships.[5] However, although these female figures do not in general have the imagined power of the old hags and crones, they are presented as being highly empathetic. Removed as they are from the patriarchal family, then, these women are not as helpless in relation to each other as natural mothers are in relation to their natural daughters, and vice versa. The relations between or among those unrelated by blood seem to have been very important in the development of female identity. Against the tenacious stereotype of women as rivals, demi-men in a play tournament, another image emerges of women as teachers and students, strangers who as universal orphans adopt each other and who learn to become mothers to themselves.

I shall begin with some courtly friends, for although the belief that developed in the utter good will and devotion of a male lover or husband eventually proved detrimental to women's friendship and unity—a belief stemming from but different than the courtly code of *fin amors*—early courts such as the Anglo-Saxon provide examples of women bonding. The male poets neither depicted nor explored these relationships to the same depth as relationships between or among men; this is as true for the gentle and ironic poet of Troyes as for the misogynistic and homo-erotic Malory.

The friendship between Iseult and Brangain, one of the more fully developed in the medieval period's poetry, displays some characteristics that almost all the friendships between women share. Moreover, at least in the presentation by Beroul, it becomes possible to sense what dangers surrounded women in the early centuries of this millenium. In Beroul's *Tristan and Iseult*, the ameliorations instituted by the women and men of Provence—the subordination, that is, of the warrior ethic to the courtly code of peace—are notably lacking.[6] Few other works expose so clearly the fear and bewilderment of people who are primitive in regard to the passions. King Marc's shifting moods and furious jealousies, Tristan's impulsive and unreasoning behavior, and Iseult's attempts to bargain for her life in a terrible desperation reveal a collective mentality at the mercy of its drives. Beroul's version of the legend suggests a social situation of unalleviated danger and brutality. Although this Anglo-Norman poet may or may not have been aware of what he was doing, his work serves as a critique of a strife-torn and power-crazed warrior culture. Beroul describes the darkest deeds starkly.

In this version of *Tristan and Iseult*, the motives for secrecy are obvious, in life as well as in artistic renderings of it. The secrecy between lady and female attendant was important not for some abstract and mannered reason, not simply to add to the excitement and intrigue of love, but because indiscretion might very well have meant death. The laws of the marriage bed were such that even if some husband were to wish to forgive an adulterous wife he was not permitted to do so.[7] Nor was actual adultery an unlikely possibility; men married women much younger than themselves and were absent from home for long periods of time, whether they were knights gone to the Crusades or merchants.[8] While there is still much debate as to how much adultery took place in fact rather than in the imaginations of poet and raconteur, the incitement to it and the feat of it most certainly did exist.[9] Both men and women risked their lives in such matters, but it was possible for men to defend themselves, while women had no recourse. Moreover, privacy was in short supply during the medieval period. Houses and castles, contrary to popular assumption, did not have many secret places; partitions were more likely to be of cloth than of wood, and one still looks forward to a work that might demonstrate the effects of such living conditions on medieval mores.[10] The lady-in-waiting, then, was privy to her mistress' affairs, both those of the toilette and those of a riskier nature.

Against this grim background, Iseult is depicted consistently as a stranger in her husband's country; she is thus without the minimal protection of a patrilocal marriage. Her guardians, brothers, uncles, or other allies of her kin are across the sea, as Beroul frequently has her bemoaning. She has been orphaned by destiny as well. The potion Iseult's mother prepared to stir the affection of King Marc and thus insure her daughter's safety has been consumed by Tristan and Iseult unwittingly before Iseult reaches her destination. Brangain, Iseult's lady-in-waiting, is charged with having confused certain vials. It is Brangain, at any rate, who becomes responsible for Iseult's safety. Estranged and at the mercy of the irrational, Iseult is almost prototypical in her helplessness. Like Chaucer's Criseyde in the Greek camp, her life is in the hands of strange men. In that part of the *Troilus*, Criseyde is altogether alone in a hostile and masculine world; in Beroul's *Tristan and Iseult*, Brangain's involvement in the fate of the heroine is constant, as are her attempts to aid and succor Iseult from the time of her culpability in the administration of the potion. Brangain, having in a sense brought the situation about, becomes and remains as responsible as a mother and puts the life of Iseult before her own.[11]

Beroul returns to this identification with and concern for the good, the peace, and the safety of the other woman at several points. Brangain's understanding of Iseult is intuitive and empathetic. In an early scene when Tristan and Iseult have barely escaped one of Marc's ambushes (Marc having tricked the lovers into meeting while he observes from the branches of a tree) Iseult returns to her chamber. Brangain is able to discern her distress immediately.

> Iseult has entered her room.
> Brangain has seen her looking pale.
> And realized that she must have had
> Some bad news
> To affect her to such an extent. . . . [12]

Brangain confronts Iseult's distress without hesitation. She asks Iseult "why she is so troubled," and Iseult replies openly, respectfully, and without reserve:

> She replies: "Oh, fair lady,
> There is good reason for my being so sad and
> Pensive.
> Brangain, I have no wish to lie to you:
> I do not know who wanted to betray us today,
> But King Marc was in the tree,
> By the big block of marble."[13]

Iseult relates the entire episode to Brangain, emphasizing in her account how both she and Tristan have tricked King Marc. Brangain's response is one of thanksgiving. Her identification with the happiness and well-being of Iseult is so complete that she comes close to blasphemy; when she hears how Tristan and Iseult have escaped from Marc she "rejoiced / Greatly."[14]

> "Iseult, my lady,
> God, who never lies, has done us a great service
> When he had you leave each other
> Without carrying matters further,
> And without the King seeing anything
> Which might be viewed in an unfavourable
> Light.
> God has performed a great miracle for you:
> He is a true Father, and as such,
> Does not want to harm
> Those who are good and faithful."[15]

The irony of calling the escape of the lovers a "miracle"—those who lie protected by a God who "never lies"—underlines Brangain's devotion. Just as the Deity is more like the God of Love than the orthodox Christian Father, and as such is partial to the lovers, Brangain will celebrate whatever force has protected the lovers. Conventional morality has been dispensed with. The safety and happiness of Iseult Brangain places at the center of her universe and before anything.

Nor does Brangain merely employ words to aid and comfort the other woman. She takes action on Iseult's behalf as well. From other versions of the story one learns that Brangain has taken Iseult's place in the marriage bed.[16] In this version, Brangain schemes to bring about a situation in which the lovers will be free to come and go as they please. When Marc commands Brangain to fetch Tristan from an inn so that the two men may be reconciled, she replies:

> "Sire, he hates me:
> In this he is very wrong, God knows.
> He says that it is because of me,
> That he has quarrelled with you;

> He is determined to seek my death.
> I shall go; for you he will give up his hatred,
> Rather than lay hands on me.
> Sire, for God's sake, reconcile me to him,
> When he has arrived here."[17]

None of the above is true, of course. Brangain concocts the fictitious quarrel to eliminate any suspicion the king might have regarding her role in the lovers' assignations. Tristan understands immediately that Brangain is making arrangements for the lovers' future meetings:

> Tristan was at the partition-wall,
> And he was able to hear them speak
> To the king.
> He has seized Brangain by the arms,
> He embraces her and gives thanks to God.
> From now on he will be free
> To be with Iseult at his pleasure.[18]

Brangain's friendship with Iseult, then, is presented as one that generates not only sympathy but action as she rescues the lovers time after time.[19]

A far more strenuous rescue operation is performed by the nurse Thessala in Chrétien de Troyes' *Cligès*, and another by a thousand ladies of the lovers' court in the same romance. This amazing composite foster-mother combines the age of a natural mother, having been with Fenice, the heroine, since her infancy, with the arcane knowledge of the old hag and the benevolence of a friend. Fenice, in a variant of the Tristan and Iseult triangle, is married to the uncle of Cligès, the hero, when the two fall in love. Because of the ministrations of Thessala, however, the lovers are not guilty of adultery, for Thessala has concocted such a potion as to cause the emperor merely to dream that he is making love to his young wife throughout their marriage. Near the climax of the tale, Fenice decides to die to the world in order to be with Cligès in utter secrecy:

And she sends for Thessala, her maid, whom she brought with her from her native land. Thessala came at once without delay, yet not knowing why she was summoned. When she asked Fenice privately what was her desire and pleasure, she concealed none of her intentions from her. "Nurse," she said, "I know full well that anything I tell you will go no further, for I have tried you thoroughly and have found you very prudent. I love you for all you have done for me. In all my troubles I appeal to you without seeking counsel elsewhere. You know why I lie awake, and what my thoughts and wishes are. My eyes behold only one object which pleases me, but I can have no pleasure or joy in it if I do not first buy it with a heavy price...." Then she told and explained to her how she was willing to feigh illness, and would complain so bitterly that at last she would pretend to be dead, and how Cliges would steal her away at night, and then they would be together all their days. She thinks that in no other way she could longer bear to live. But if she was sure that she would consent to lend her aid, the matter would be arranged in accordance with their wishes. "But I am tired of waiting for me joy and luck." Then the nurse assured her that she would help her in every way, telling her to have no further fear. She said that as soon as she set to work she would bring it about that there would be no man, upon seeing her, who would not certainly believe that the soul had left the body after she had drunk of a potion which would leave her cold, colourless, pale, and stiff, without power of speech and deprived of health; yet she would be alive and well, and would have no sensations of any kind, and would be none the worse for a day and a night entire spent in the sepulchre and bier.[20]

The trusty Thessala indeed prepares such a potion and takes preliminary measures as well to insure the credibility of Fenice's pretended demise. There is, however, a snag in the plot, as three physicians from Salerno appear at Fenice's funeral and, unable to believe that she is dead, undertake to bring her to by cajoling her, then beating her, and then cajoling her again. They are about to kill her, in fact, in their efforts to make her react when she is rescued by the ladies of the court and Thessala:

Thus the miserable villains torment and afflict the lady, by taking the lead all boiling hot from the fire and pouring it into the palms of her hands. Not satisfied with pouring the lead clean through her palms, the cowardly rascals say that, if she does not speak at once, they will straightway stretch her completely on the grate until she is completely grilled. Yet, she holds her peace and does not refuse to have her body beaten and maltreated by them. Now they were on the point of placing her upon the fire to be roasted and grilled when more than a thousand ladies, who were stationed before the palace, come to the door and through a little crack catch sight of the torture and anguish which they were inflicting upon the lady, as with coal and flame they accomplished her martyrdom. They bring clubs and hammers to smash and break down the door. Great was the noise and uproar as they battered and broke in the door. If now they can lay their hands on the doctors, the latter will not have long to wait before they receive their full deserts. With a single rush the ladies enter the palace, and in the press is Thessala, who has no other aim but to reach her mistress. Beside the fire she finds her stripped, severely wounded and injured. She puts her back on the bier again, and over her she spreads a cloth, while the ladies go to give their reward to the three doctors, without wishing to wait for the emperor or his seneschal. Out of the windows they threw them down into the courtyard, breaking the necks, ribs, arms, and legs of all: no better piece of work was ever done by any ladies.[21]

Charmed as one is by the tone of this action against respected members of the medical profession, one should not overlook Thessala's restoration of Fenice to life.

Several queens are depicted in the romance literature as fostering the young women who serve them, albeit in a less dramatic manner. In *Floris and Blanchefleur*, the queen who does so acts in a more responsible way than the girl's natural mother. The queen in this widely circulated French tale—translated into English in the thirteenth century—has in effect adopted Blanchefleur and also saves her from certain death. As queen of the heathen court of Almeria, she has taken in the young girl, the daughter of a lady captive, and brings her up, educating her together with her own son, Floris. The two children love each other so much that the king thinks he must have Blanchefleur put to death in order for his son to marry properly, that is, for his son to marry one of his own station.

> The king understood the great love
> Between his son and Blanchefleur,
> And thought, when they came of age,
> That their love would not cease,
> Nor that Floris would be able to withdraw
> His love when he should marry after the law.
> The king then took the queen aside
> And told her what was troubling him,
> Of his thought and of his worry
> How Floris in the future would fare.
> "Dame," he said, "I'll tell you my plan:

> I wish Blanchefleur be put to death,
> And when that maiden is slain
> And no more life within her,
> As soon as Floris accepts this,
> He will forget her;
> Then he may marry in proper fashion."[22]

To this gentle suggestion the queen responds by thinking how to "save the maiden from death," for although she, too, would like to see her son marry one of his own rank, she is unwilling to see Blanchefleur murdered.

> "Sir," she said, "certainly we ought to see
> That Florent lives quite properly
> To his estate and that he won't lose
> His honor, for the maiden Blanchefleur;
> It would be better if someone else
> Took that cleanly maiden, than to bring her
> To death; it would be much more honorable
> Than slaying her. . . ."[23]

The queen suggests another plan, which is fairly complicated and deceitful but will not entail the shedding of blood. She suggests that Floris be sent away for some time to her own sister, living at a distance; there, she thinks, his ardor will cool. In the meantime, he must be told that Blanchefleur's mother is ill and that therefore the girl cannot join him.[24]

The queen's suggestion is followed, but Floris when kept from his sweetheart begins to waste away. The king, concerned with his son only, once more seeks Blanchefleur's death, and in a more adamant manner. He learns of his son's poor health in a letter:

> The king immediately broke the seal
> In order to know what the letter imported.
> His mood began to change,
> As he soon understood what had happened,
> And in wrath he called the queen,
> Told her of his grief,
> And with anger he now spoke and said:
> "Let that maid be brought forth!
> From her body her head shall go."[25]

The queen again resists and proposes a second scheme. She would send Blanchefleur away with some slave-traders, and although this may seem almost as cruel as the king's scheme, the notion of sending a child away in order to save it is an idea at least as old as the story of Moses. For when the queen hears what the king intends, she is "ful woo," full of woe.

> Then the queen spoke, that good lady:
> "For God's love, sir, have mercy!
> At the next harbor hereabouts
> There are, I know, rich traders—
> Prosperous merchants from Babylon
> Who would gladly buy her.
> Then you will profit from the lovely account,
> And have much in the way of possessions and goods,
> And in that way she may be taken from us
> So that we will not have to slay her."[26]

Thus the poet here juxtaposes the blithe bloodthirstiness of the king, and his concern for the welfare of his son alone, with the queen's efforts to save the girl, a strange child. It is she who convinces her husband that life is more important than the expediency with which he wishes to uphold the royal *status quo*. It is the queen who dissuades Floris from committing suicide after he hears of Blanchefleur's supposed death. It is she who pleads with the king, and who pleads for mercy as one who has experienced the truth of the childbed.

> Forth the queen came running, weeping,
> Until she reached the king.
> And then that good lady said:
> "For God's love, sir, have mercy!
> Out of the twelve children born to us
> None are alive except this one,
> And it would be better if she were his mate
> Than if her were to die for her sake."[27]

This kind of fellow-feeling is echoed in the same work in the friendship between Blanchefleur and another young woman. When Blanchefleur has been sold into slavery, and is taken away as is usual in these tales to the mysterious East,[28] in the court of a prince there she experiences the comfort of her friendship with one Clarice. The poet describes this relationship. When Floris arrives secretly, he startles Clarice who, however,

> understood right away
> That this was Blanchefleur's sweetheart;
> For their bowers were close together
> And they seldom were far apart,
> And each knew the other's counsel,
> And each in the other trusted much.[29]

Here, where both maidens are well-nigh helpless in their captivity, they are taking care of each other. Rivalry between them is not mentioned, as the following scene will illustrate.

With the same acute and immediate understanding that appeared in the depiction of Brangain, Clarice takes the responsibility of testing Blanchefleur's fidelity and steadfastness. She tells Blanchefleur that a lovely flower awaits her, which signifies that a lover has come. Blanchefleur declares that she will not change her old love for a new, whereupon Clarice, satisfied with this response, leads Blanchefleur to her sweetheart. The two lovers recognize and embrace; but now they must rely upon Clarice to guard their secret.

> Both of these sweet things in their bliss
> Fell down to kiss her feet,
> And cried to her, weeping, that
> For mercy she would not betray them
> To the king, for if they were betrayed
> They would most certainly be dead.[30]

The lovers thus depend on her for their lives. Then, the poet relates, Clarice addresses Blanchefleur with words full of fine and courtly feeling:

> "You need not fear any more
> Than if this had happened to me.
> And you must know certainly
> That I will help you in your plight."[31]

Clarice identifies with the other woman completely. Blanchefleur's trouble is her trouble, and what is even more enchanting, Blanchefleur's joy is her joy.

This desire to aid, comfort, and abet, as in the case of Brangain and Iseult, stimulates Clarice's wit. Identification and solicitude again prompt quick thinking when danger to the other is at hand. When the king asks why Blanchefleur is not present on the morning after the lovers have been reunited, an immediate excuse springs to the lips of Blanchefleur's friend. One notes the tenderness of the little scene that precedes the moment of danger:

> Clarice, as she was wont to do,
> Got up in the morning and called
> To Blanchefleur to come with her
> To the tower. Blanchefleur said,
> "I'm coming," so Clarice went her way,
> Thinking that Blanchefleur had heeded.
> As soon as Clarice got to the tower,
> The Ameral asked for Blanchefleur.
> "Sire," she said right away,
> "She has been awake all night,
> And she prayed and looked about,
> And she read somewhat in her book,
> And she made to God her plea
> That He give you His blessing
> And that you would live very long;
> Now she is sleeping so soundly,
> That sweet maiden Blanchefleur,
> That she hasn't been able to come yet."[32]

Clarice, then, during Blanchefleur's captivity in the Ameral's court, protects her friend under dangerous circumstances and in ways which Floris, the lover, cannot emulate.

I shall discuss the plight of solitary women who must depend upon individual men at another point; that dependency aside, here and there we find indications of women dependent on their women friends to a much greater extent than we are accustomed, not only in the romances but also in the homeliest British texts. Chaucer, too, alludes to this in

The Legend of Good Women when Thisbe, alone in the night, begins
to regret her decision to run away with a man.

> For alle hire frendes—for to save hire trouthe—
> She hath forsake; allas! and that is routhe
> That evere woman wolde ben so trewe
> To truste man, but she the bet hym knewe![33]

While this does not allude to women friends, it does refer to a conflict
obscured by centuries of a male-centered ethos between the need for the
protection and strength of other women and allegiance to the lover or
husband. The popular imagination has managed to recognize this
conflict; in the South English *Nativity of Mary and Christ*, for example,
when Joseph returns home from the Temple to find his wife with child,
the virgins whom he has brought in to stay with her cluster round to
assure the irate Joseph that nothing untoward has happened in his
absence. His anger, they assure him, has no foundation; and the preg-
nancy is "free from guilt."

> "For your wife is chaste and good—
> We know nothing but that of her;
> She never spoke in private
> With any man we were aware of."[34]

Protection and support here come not from the husband, of course, in
his fear of having been cuckolded, but from a group of women as young
as Mary herself.

The best example of the conflict, albeit in a comic and exaggerated
form, is to be found in the play *Noah's Flood*, of the Chester watermen.
Although one editor has called Noah's wife "a shrew and an obstruc-
tionist,"[35] her concern for the well-being of her "gossips" is not altogether unpraiseworthy. When Noah bids her enter the Ark, she replies:

> Yea, sir, go on! Set up your sail,
> And then row forth into the gale.
> But I stay here, for, without fail,
> I will not leave this town.

> Unless thou tak'st my gossips on,
> Not one more foot will I be gone.
> If they must drown, then, by St. John,
>   I will not save my life.
> They love me well. I do not jest.
> Take them with me into thy chest,
> Or else row forth and do thy best
>   To get thee a new wife.[36]

We are supposed to laugh at Noah's wife's refusal to board the Ark, of course, at her willingness to let her sons and husband go off, at the way in which she is bundled onto the Ark by the three boys, and at how she delivers to Noah a resounding slap, because she is to appear so short-sighted that she would rather remain, drink and drown with her gossips than sail away with her family, the original nuclear family, as it were. It is highly comic and certainly as in the best comedy permits a recognition perhaps too painful for any other mode.[37]

Even Guenevere, in some ways the loneliest heroine in English litera-ture, in the Old French *La Mort du Roi Artu* depends upon another woman to save her from certain death at the most crucial moment of her crisis-ridden life. Her dilemma is, as she tells a cousin, that her "lord the king"

> "has undertaken this battle and if Mordred wins, he will kill me. If my lord is victorious he will not believe at all that Mordred has not known me carnally, because of the great force he exerted to have me; I know truly he will kill me as soon as he can lay hands on me. By this double reasoning you can see clearly that I cannot escape death either from one side or from the other."[38]

Whereas in Malory Launcelot comes to the rescue at this juncture, in the French version the queen seeks help of a different kind, in the world of women:

> That night the queen rested but little, as she was not at ease, but badly frightened, for she saw safety nowhere. The next day, as soon as it was light, she waked two of her damsels, the ones in whom she had the greatest confidence. When they were dressed and ready, she had each mount on

her palfrey, took two squires with her, and caused two pack animals laden
with gold and silver to be led out of the tower. So the queen quitted London
and went to a forest nearby, where there was an abbey of nuns that her
ancestors had established.[39]

Guenevere addresses her damsels before she enters:

> "If you like, damsels, you may go away, and if you like you may remain.
> As for me, I tell you that I shall stay here and will enter religion among the
> nuns here, for my mother, who was queen of Tarnelide, and considered a
> virtuous lady, came here and lived out the rest of her life."[40]

But, as it turns out, as Guenevere has cared for her damsels, the damsels
will care for her and they refuse to leave her side.

The following scene Ma¹ ᵧ eliminates completely. It is a dialogue
between Guenevere and the abbess. When Guenevere enters, the abbess
"showed her very great joy" and the queen requests admission to the
order:

> "My lady," said the abbess, "if the king had passed on from this world,
> we would very gladly make you one of our ladies and our companion. But
> because he still lives, we would not dare to receive you, for he would
> certainly kill us, as soon as he found it out, and, besides, my lady, there is
> something else. I am sure that if we had received you, you would not be
> able to hold up under our rules, for there is much severity in them, especial-
> ly for you who have had all the comforts in the world."[41]

In other words, the abbess, although friendly to Guenevere, is loathe to
accept her because such acceptance would imperil her own life and the
life of the nuns for whom she is responsible. At this point the queen tries
to intimidate the abbess:

> "My lady," said the queen, "If you do not receive me, it will be the worse
> for you and for me, for if I go on from here, and evil by chance befalls me,
> the misfortune will be mine, but the king will ask you for my body, be sure
> of that, for by your fault I will have suffered evil."[42]

But the abbess is not to be intimidated. Only when Guenevere appeals
to her fellow-feeling and pity does the abbess change her mind:

> The queen spoke so long to the abbess that the latter did not know what
> to say. The queen drew her aside, and told her of the anguish and fear,
> because of which she wanted to enter religion.[43]

Hearing this account, the abbess resolves to accept Guenevere and also
conceives a plan for keeping the nuns safe from the king's ire:

> "My lady," said the abbess, "here is what I advise. You will stay here,
> yes, and if by ill luck Mordred overcomes King Arthur and wins this battle,
> then you may appropriately take our habit and enter our order completely.
> If the God of Glory should give your lord victory in this battle and he
> gained the upper hand and returned here safe and sound, I would make
> your peace with him, and you would be better received by him than you
> ever were."[44]

The queen respectfully replies that she will do whatever the "good and
loyal" abbess counsels.

In this episode, women do not behave in stereotyped fashion. Guenevere first thinks of seeking help from other women, and her own ladies-in-
waiting rally around her in an evil time. Guenevere is concerned for the
well-being of these "damsels," and she shows respect for their lives. The
abbess is gladdened by Guenevere's approach, yet clearly perceives the
danger inherent in the situation. She decides, in full knowledge of that
danger, to protect Guenevere as well as the women in her charge. She is
portrayed as tolerant and far from harsh, although she herself is living
under a severe rule. Here, one woman rescues another; Guenevere is
adopted by a true Mother Superior.

From Anglo-Saxon times, nuns, abbesses, and other religious women
living away from the family and outside the patriarchal structure proper,
though able to provide a certain amount of support and shelter, were
never completely autonomous and were subject—as in the literary passage
quoted—to political pressure and the censure of the higher (male) clergy.
At no time in the medieval period did the orders of women have anything
like the power of the male religious houses.[45]

Nonetheless, women in the convents seem to have been freer in certain
ways than women isolated in castle halls.[46] Convent rules, according to
one writer, were less severe than those of the monasteries. Perhaps this

was so because less was expected of women, but perhaps also the function of the female authorities was not so much to discipline as to succor.[47] At the close of the medieval period, when so-called corruption was rampant, investigation of some nunneries revealed that a good number of women within them were pregnant. The abbesses had not revealed the state of these nuns to the authorities.[48] Although the lack of corrective action may be regarded as permissive, corrupt, or motivated by shame and fear, it might also indicate an understanding of the diverse purposes involved in the founding and upkeep of religious houses for women, a tacit admission that women entered for shelter and for a life outside the patriarchal family structure as well as for religious reasons.[49]

This lack of harshness in nuns' rules of the Anglo-Saxon period is encouraged by the Venerable Bede.[50] In *The Tradition of the Nun in Medieval England*, Sister Mary Byrne summarizes Bede's thought on the superior.

> As superior of a community the abbess' great care is directed to the provision of all that her subjects need; hence, both in a spiritual and in a material sense the abbess merits the title, Mother, a term of affection and reverence applied frequently to the abbesses of whom Bede writes. One, he remarks, is mother not only to her vast community but to all who know her, so all-embracing is her devotion and solicitude. Nuns call the abbess "My most dear Mother" and Venerable Bede describes one as "A careful Mother," the "Mother and Nurse of consecrated women"; another, "The virgin Mother of many nuns." So genuine, reverent and ardent is filial affection which the abbess wins that it seems no less spontaneous than that enjoyed by one abbess who is actually "the mother of one of her nuns."[51]

In a note on this passage, Sister Byrne remarks that "Whether or not 'Mother' was an official designation for a religious superior at that time is beside the point. The context of the term in Bede implies in the case of all these women a tribute to their mother-like solicitude."[52]

Anglo-Saxon society, however, was in many ways more egalitarian than later medieval society.[53] One might question whether what Sister Byrne calls the "abbess-tradition" with its sense of motherly responsibility and care persisted. I would venture that it did indeed remain the model for the later period and, furthermore, that as women in secular life are represented as more and more male-centered, the religious figure as mother-surrogate in the literature stands out in greater relief.

Many *vitae* of the medieval period are redactions of earlier material, the details retained acquiring additional significance. Moreover, there are not one but two collections of female saints' lives in English. As a late nineteenth-century editor put it:

> Twice in the earlier English (and no other) literature, was an attempt made to put together the lives of female saints: by Bokenham in verse, and in the present collection—a peculiar instance of the veneration which the weaker part of mankind, especially in its godlike members, enjoys in this island.[54]

The two collections illustrate not only the veneration and respect that may have been accorded female saints—in line with the Anglo-Saxon hagiographical tradition—but an attempt, unconscious or otherwise, to provide women with models of feminine conduct, an attempt to provide them with a group of symbolic fostermothers to compensate for the absence or weakness of the actual mothers. Indeed, the second collection, compiled about 1610 by a Catholic author living in a Protestant time, seems an attempt to replace the actual mothers with the saints of purely Catholic times,[55] and a firmly Catholic tradition of hagiography.

The seventeenth-century author of *The Lives of Women Saints of our Countrie of England* heavily emphasizes virginity once more and in his preface is quite straightforward on this subject. Since "the liues following principallie concerne Virgins and widowes," he writes, he invokes St. Cyprian's authority on virginity:

> Virginnes (sayeth he) are the floure of the Churche seede, the honor and ornament of spiritual grace, the moste towardlie impes, the intire and incorrupt worke of praise and honor, the image of God, resembling our lordes holiness (who was a virgin) and the most worthie portion of Christ flocke: By them and in them dooth the glorious fertilities of our mother the Church greatlie reioyce, and aboundantlyie flourish: and how much the more in number virgins augment and multiplie, so much the more dooth our mothers comfort and increase.[56]

In the quotations from authority, this author would retain the image of the mother as the model for female behavior but dispense with the entire process of natural generation:

> Keepe virgins, keepe safe I pray you, that which you haue begunne, that which you are to be in tyme. A greate reward is kept for you, a mightie price for virtue, the highest payment for chastitie. Will you vnderstand what euills continencie wanteth, and what commodities it conteyneth: *I will multiplie* (sayd God to the woman) *thy griefes and sorrowes, with greate paine shalt thou beare thy children, thou shalt be conuerted to thy husband, and he shall be thy lorde*. You virgins are free from this sentence, you feare not the sorrowes and paynfull trauailes of mothers, you neede not be awfull of the griefes sutayned in childebearing; neither is a mortall man your maister, but your maister and head is Christ, as he is of men also: you are now equall with them in freedome.[57]

These are teachings and arguments encountered before in *Hali Meidenhad*, but here the author reasons more self-consciously:

> The first commandement at the creation of the worlde, was to increase and multiplie; but the second (at our regeneration by Christ) persuadeth continencie. When the world was rude and emptie, by fertilitie and generation multitude was procured: but the world now being replenished, they that can get chastitie and liue single like Eunuches, are so spiritually gelded for the kingdome of heaven.[58]

The author of *Hali Meidenhad* urged his female readers to chastity first by denigrating earthly marriage and especially motherhood, then by offering Christ as the perfect spouse, but he did not offer any female or maternal models for the women to follow.[59] This author seems to be offering his female readers *wombless* mothers. The model of mother-daughter is retained in the relationships he presents, but the female figures of greatest strength are not the natural mothers of natural daughters within the legends; instead they are the tutelary abbesses, the heads of convents, the strong-willed and celibate saints themselves. In this way, the author attempts to resolve the dilemma of female identification we have encountered before.[60] He endeavors to give women who will not bear children mothers who have not borne children as models of true womanhood, and thus to meet the identity problem of a daughter who is not also a mother.

Not that this author has done away with natural mothers completely. On the contrary, in several lives, the mothers themselves bring their daughters to the convents or monasteries:

> A certain noble woman of Scotland had a daughter which had been mute from her natiuite; the mother brought her to Brigide, who taking her by the hand, asked her if for the loue of Christ, she would keepe her self chaste perpetuallie: see a wonder: She presentlie hauing her tongue losed, did answer that she would moste promptlie doe, whatsoeuer she would will her.[61]

Whole dynasties are founded in this way, the mothers and their daughters embracing spiritual motherhood and daughterhood. Sexburge, for example, brings up all her children to "reuerence, to feare and serue god," particularly her daughter Erkengoda, who "went beyond the seas, to professe her self a religious woman, and there in the monasterie of Briga, shined with great holinesse and many miracles."[62] Sexburge herself, after her husband's death, "cast away all the pompe and rioting of the worlde, and tooke the religious habit of professed chastitie and sanctimonie in the Abbie of Elie, subjecting her self for Christs sake vnto her sister St. Ethelred of Audrie Abbesse then and founder of that Nonnerie."[63]

Grandmothers, too, the author recounts, give themselves to the religious life in these celibate communities. When Queen Ermenilde's husband had died,

> by whose help she wrought that former promotion of gods glorie, she ceased not in an other kinde to edifie all, that was by example: teaching them to contemne the worlde, and moste feruentlie to runne towards heauen. For with her daughter Werburge (whose life followeth) she forsook the glorie and vaine pompe of this life, and entred into the monasterie of Elie, where her mother Sexburge was, but her sister Audrie Abbesse. . . .[64]

At this point the author glosses the text ecstatically: "O what a glorious societie, the grandmother, mother and neece, all religious together and Saints: and the Abbesse Aunt and a Sainte."[65]

The point of these family chronicles seems to involve the hagiographer's commitment to keeping the mothers within the narrative structures, for it is finally the mothers who permit, accede to, and approve of their daughters' transference of loyalties. This becomes clear in "The Life of St. Macrina," in which an old mother, on her deathbed, wills her daughter to the Church:

> "To thee Lord doe I dedicate the first and last, which is also the tenth fruite of my wombe: this daughter first begotten, is my first fruite. . . ."[66]

Some mothers even dream of their daughters becoming saints while they are in the womb; they then dedicate them to the religious life and turn them over to mother-surrogates. In such a way, St. Keyna was destined for sanctity

> before she was borne, being in her mother's bellie, and her future holinesse foresignified: For her mother in a vision, beheld her wombe replenished and her papps to shine with heauenly light.[67]

Nor are the expectations of the natural mothers—according to this text —disappointed. The abbesses here do indeed nurture, protect, and teach, in the early legends and in the later ones. For example, St. Ethelburge's religious education is described in the following terms: her brother, wishing to keep her in her own country, "prouided for her a spirituall teacher named Hildelitha, a woman as well excellentlie learned in the liberall sciences, as verie expert, in skill of religious discipline and life."[68] He builds a convent for them and "placed them there with other virgins,"[69] so providing Ethelburge with the opportunity to become a surrogate mother in her turn:

> This virgin in short time surpassed all others farre in all vertue and holynes, and at last was chosen mother or Abbesse of them all. . . . She preached and exhorted her Sisters without ceasing to all contempt of this world, teaching them to abhorre the vanitie and corruption therof. . . .[70]

She comforts them in time of plague and teaches them to endure great suffering. The quality of reciprocity in these women's relationships is stressed.

One of the sisters named Torgitha, that had beene wasted by nyne yeares sicknes, in a vision of a glorious bedd carried vp into heauen, in triumphant manner, vnderstood that her mother Ethelburge was shortlie to leaue this life, for attayning of a better, which indeede so fell oute: But afterward she did not requite Torgitha with like charitie, for when she dyed Ethelburge appeared vnto her and tolde her she was come to fetch her to heuenliche ioyes; whereat Torgitha yielding her moste hartie thankes, withal yielded vp her religious spirite.[71]

These saintly generations of surrogate mothers and daughters exclude one female figure of extreme importance: Mary, the Mother of God. Mary is a highly problematic figure in this context in that not only is she a mother—virginal or not—but she is worshipped because she is a mother. Albeit the mother of a son, Mary has given birth to Christ, and therefore her womb cannot really be denigrated.[72]

The legends referred to as "Miracles of the Virgin" encompass a wide range of attitudes, demonstrating the problem of Mary to different degrees. Chaucer's Prioress, for example, is made to dedicate her tale to the Virgin Mother, "the white lylye flour" who "is a mayde alway."[73] This "moder Mayde" and mayde Mooder free"[74] is, in a very particular and biological sense, just what the Prioress cannot be. The Prioress at first expresses the wish to be as a little child, "of twelf month oold, or lesse,"[75] and indeed her moral awareness seems to have been arrested at an early stage.[76] She is made to be obsessed, furthermore, with motherhood throughout the tale: only ten of the twenty-nine stanzas in the tale contain no reference to mother or child. In the rest, both the "litel clergeoun" and his mother and the Virgin Mother appear again and again. The very air of the tale resounds with celebration of Mary as Mother. The child sings his *Alma redemptoris* in honor of "Oure blisful Lady, cristes mooder deere," "Oure Lady," Christ's "mooder, honour of mankynde," and "This welle of mercy, Cristes mooder sweete."[77] The Prioress, however, cannot be a mother in the literal sense and in her literal-mindedness is not really able to identify with Mary's qualities of pity and compassion, the "moodres pitee" she speaks of.[78] Her bloodthirsty tirade against the Jews, for example, suggests a Chaucerian discernment of the link between frustration and violence, and of what imperfect identifications might be provoked by the paradox of the Immaculate Conception on those women dedicated to virginity.

The Virgin Mother frequently enters directly into the Miracles and comes to the aid of women in distress, including those wrongfully accused of infidelity.[79] In *The Empress of Rome*, for example, the emperor's brother, lusting after the empress, is rejected by her, at which point he accuses her to the king of having tried to seduce him.[80] The emperor delivers his wife to an executioner and, although she is saved by a knight who makes her the nurse of his child, fate has another misfortune in store for her. Wooed by a yeoman at the new court, whose advances she also refuses, she finds that the yeoman has slit the throat of the child she is caring for.[81] The knight then has the empress bound and thrown into the sea:

> But by Our Lady's great might,
> The waves held her upright,
> In the sea to and fro,
> So that she was not born to the bottom.[82]

A fisherman rescues her from the water and leaves her on the shore, where "When she was alone there, / She prayed to Our Lady especially / To help her in her great need."[83] The Virgin Mother appears, bearing a plant:

> "Empress," she said, "do not worry:
> You shall have this plant.
> You shall be able to save all lepers
> That acknowledge in open confession
> All their sins.
> Go home to your own country;
> Your enemies will be lepers.
> And they must declare
> So that everyone shall see and hear,
> That they falsely accused you
> In anger and distemper.
> After that you shall immediately
> Heal each of them."[84]

The empress, following the Virgin's instructions, finally convinces the emperor of her virtue and becomes his wife once again:

When the Emperoure saw
That high miracle
Done so graciously
By the might of Our Lady,
And saw the goodness of his wife,
That had so cleanly lead her life,
He took her with good will.
He went with her to the pope
And he received of the pope a pardon
For what he had done amiss,
And he lived happily with her forever
Until God took them both away.[85]

This Miracle, imbued as it is with the quality of fantasy and wish-fulfillment, has rescue as its predominant theme and image. The empress is saved from the executioner's hands, from the court of the knight, from the waves of the sea. She, in turn, saves. She nurses the knight's orphaned child, heals the sick, and finally cures the emperor's soul. Salvation in the sense of rescue is the particular function of the Virgin Mother, so much so that in Herolt's *Miracles of the Blessed Virgin Mary* one begins to wonder about Mary's divine status. All who call upon the Mother for help in their time of need receive it, and it seems her power is thus limited by her mercy and limitless compassion.[86] But this is as it must be, as Mary is mother-love incarnate, all-accepting and nonjudgemental. Moreover, the fantasy of rescue, Helene Deutsch has written, is one of the most common fantasies of mothering on the part of adoptive mothers and stepmothers.[87]

We also see that the empress is threatened throughout this work by men. The pattern of these accusations is interesting and revealing in and of itself. The empress is endangered by the projected desires of her would-be suitors. This work thus represents a very common medieval psychological phenomenon, in which women are seen as more sexual than men because of men's fears for their own sexuality.[88] That the empress is threatened by what the men see as her sexuality relates this text to those in which an old hag appears in tandem with another, younger woman. There is also an alliance in *The Empress of Rome* of woman with woman, foster mother and adopted daughter; the nature of the daughter-figure's sexual ends is here of central importance.

It differs of course in the redemptive nature of the daughter-figure's desires, in the very motherly nature of her deeds. One may well smile at the small stroke of vengeance. The Virgin Mother is not above making all of the empress' enemies sick before they can be cured.[89] However, they will be cured if they repent. The Virgin appears to the empress when she is alone; woman to woman, then, the Virgin instructs, teaches the empress how she must save even her enemies in order to save herself. She must in particular save her husband, who is presented here as ignorant, not malevolent, if both are to thrive. Mothering, then, is here the model of conduct for women, and an active, redemptive mothering at that. One notes finally that the Virgin bears a plant. Is this not symbolic of the magic power in fruition, the power of the woman to give life? Several of the old women considered—the witch Agostes, for example —are also depicted as having the power of healing. In fact, herbal cures and remedies were virtually the only ones employed by women of the Middle Ages when they "doctored." The plant, then, seems to represent the healing power of woman in her mothering role.

The Empress of Rome actually sets forth a very positive image of foster mothers and foster daughters. The salvation of men is seen as the desired goal of women, as the task passes from mother to daughter. The Virgin Mother teaches here by example. She is the mother of and Intercessor for all human beings. The empress, queen of the earth just as Mary is Queen of Heaven, identifies with the mother figure completely in this role.

The Virgin does not always present women with such an affirmative view of themselves, however, nor is she always as potent in what she can accomplish. Sister Mary Gripkey discusses the Virgin's place in the heavenly hierarchy:

> An investigation of the miracula reveals the following facts: the miracles of the twelfth and thirteenth centuries do not differ in the matter of theocentrism from those in the preceding centuries; no collection has been found which does not present the Blessed Virgin in the secondary role of suppliant, dependent upon the will of God for the favor she wishes to bestow upon a client.
>
> . . . divine omnipotence, manifested in the miracles of the Old Testament is repeatedly said to be displayed again in those legends in which the Virgin takes an active part.[90]

In other words, even the Miracles of the Virgin exist within the framework of patriarchal thought and belief.

Thus, in the role of mother to her earthly daughters Mary may present the image of supplicant or urge her daughters themselves to take on that guise, as in the image of the mantle of meekness. In *The Revelations of Saint Birgitta*, a late medieval work, the "mother of God" speaks directly to Birgitta on several occasions, and in one instance delivers this particular image to the saint.[91] "I am called by all," Mary relates, "the mother of mercy."

> In truth, daughter, the mercy of my son made me merciful, and his suffering made me to have compassion. . . . Therefore, you, my daughter, come and hide under my mantle, which is outwardly despicable but inwardly is beneficial for three things. First, it shelters from tempestuous winds. Secondly, it keeps from biting cold. Thirdly, it defends from rain. This mantle is my meekness.[92]

So she advises Birgitta to gain strength from self-abasement, to seek a shelter in gentleness, and a place to hide from the cruelty and strife of the world. This seems the most likely counsel a medieval mother or mother surrogate could give. Even the Queen of Heaven could only supplicate her Son on behalf of her daughters; and the passive, protective virtues must have appeared the most effective, not to mention the safest. The example of meekness, a genuine and general Christian virtue, must have provided women with a style of survival, emotional as well as physical, throughout the centuries; but it has made it more difficult for them in succeeding generations to change their lot.

A most remarkable surrogate mother appears in the work of the great English mystic, Julian of Norwich. Julian as other mystic writers employs the language of the senses in order to convey a personal, individual experience of the divine. In *The Revelations of Divine Love*, however, what is inherent in the language of the early revelations becomes full-blown doctrine in the later ones.[93] Extraordinary in these is Julian's unfolding revelation of God as feminine, the explicit making-over of the Father and Son in the female image, and the transformation of the persons of the patriarchal trinity into motherhood incarnate.

It is no accident that the mystic who accomplishes this is herself a woman. Much Judeo-Christian mysticism does indeed admit of the female component in the godhead, but Julian goes much farther. In this work, *The Revelations*, Julian in the first vision begins somewhat conventionally with Mary as Mother: "I saw her ghostly, in bodily likeness: a simple maid and a meek, young in age and little waxen above a child, in the stature that she was when she conceived with child."[94] But it is not only in the passages that deal explicitly with Mary that images of conception, birth, and early care appear. The Lord, for example, Julian writes, in "his homely loving,"

> is to us everything that is good and comfortable for us. He is our clothing that for love wrappeth us, claspeth us, and all becloseth us for tender love, that he may never leave us. . . .[95]

Other images of enclosure and embrace follow.

> For as the body is clad in the cloth, and the flesh in the skin, and the bones in the flesh, and the heart in the whole, so are we, soul and body, clad in the Goodness of God, and enclosed.[96]

After Julian's dark night of the soul, her terrible fever and agony, indicative of inner ambivalence and strife, Jesus grants her a vision of his Mother:

> And with this same cheer of mirth and joy our good Lord looked down on the right side and brought to my mind where our Lady stood in the time of his Passion; and said: "Wilt thou see her?" And in this sweet word it was as if he had said: "I wot well thou wouldst see my blessed Mother: for, after myself, she is the highest joy that I might shew thee, and most liking and worship to me; and most she is desired to be seen of my blessed creatures." And for the high, marvellous, singular love that he hath to this sweet Maiden, his blessed Mother, our Lady Saint Mary, he shewed her highly rejoicing as by the meaning of these sweet words; as if said: "Wilt thou see how I love her, that thou mightest joy with me in the love that I have in her and she in me?"[97]

It is by "the virtues of her blessed soul," Julian relates, "her truth, her wisdom, her charity; whereby I may learn to know myself and reverently dread my God."[98] Jesus' laudation of his Mother, that is, opens her way to acceptance of herself.

Julian does not stop with the acceptance of the woman and mother as the mother of Christ. She returns in the fifty-fourth chapter to images of enclosure, of motherhood, of bearing a child in the womb:

> For the Almighty Truth of the Trinity is our Father: for he made us and keepeth us in him; and the deep Wisdom of the Trinity is our Mother, in whom we are all enclosed; the high Goodness of the Trinity is our Lord, and in him we are enclosed, and he in us. We are enclosed in the Father, and we are enclosed in the Son, and we are enclosed in the Holy Ghost. And the Father is enclosed in us, and the Son is enclosed in us: Almightiness, All-Wisdom, All-Goodness: one God, one Lord.[99]

Chapter fifty-eight presents a further development of the maternal imagery and a shift of the most radical kind:

> And furthermore I saw that the Second Person, which is our Mother as anent the Substance, that same dearworthy Person is become our Mother as anent the Sense-soul. For we are doubly in God's making: that is to say, Substantial and Sensual. Our Substance is the highter part, which we have in our Father, God Almighty; and the Second Person of the Trinity is our Mother in kind, in making of our Substance, in whom we are grounded and rooted. And he is our Mother in Mercy, in our Sensuality taking. And thus our Mother is to us in diverse manners working: in whom our parts are kept undisparted.[100]

Dame Julian becomes even more definite:

> Thus Jesus Christ that doeth good against evil is our very Mother: we have our Being of him—where the ground of Motherhood beginneth —with all the sweet Keeping of Love that endlessly followeth. As verily as God is our Father, so verily God is our Mother. . . .[101]

And she elaborates further:

> But now behoveth to say a little more of this forthspreading, as I understand in the meaning of our Lord: how that we be brought again by the Motherhood of Mercy and Grace into our Nature's place, where that we were made by the Motherhood of kind Love: which Kindly-Love, it never leaveth us.

Our Kind Mother, our Gracious Mother, for that he would all wholly become our Mother in all things, he took the ground of his Works full low and full mildly in the Maiden's womb. . . . That is to say: our high God is sovereign Wisdom of all: in this low place he arrayed and dight him full ready in our poor flesh, himself to do the service and the office of Motherhood in all things.[102]

For Julian of Norwich, Jesus' love *is* Mother-love, the model and source of all love. "The Mother's service is nearest, readiest, and surest: for it is most of truth."[103] Her imagination quickens and warms to the notion so that she may now substantiate it:

The mother may give her child suck of her milk, but our precious Mother, Jesus, he may feed us with himself. . . . The mother may lay the child tenderly to her breast, but our tender Mother, Jesus, he may homely lead us into his blessed breast, by his sweet open side. . . .[104]

A great distance has been traveled between Plato, for example, and his denigration of the feminine in the formation of the cosmos and Julian's conception:

This fair lovely word *Mother*, it is so sweet and so kind itself that it may not verily be said of none but him; and to her that is the Mother of him and of all. To the property of Motherhood belongth kind love, wisdom, and knowing; and it is good: The kind, loving Mother that witteth and knoweth the need of her child, she keepeth it full tenderly, as the kind and condition of Motherhood will. And as it waxeth in age, she changeth her working, but not her love. And when it is waxen of more age, she suffereth that it be beaten in breaking down of vices, to make the child receive virtues and graces.[105]

Julian of Norwich reshapes the universe, recreating the image of the godhead to include her own image. By including Motherhood in God, as a daughter of this God, she becomes the creator of her mother, and a mother to herself.

The greatest fostermother in the medieval period is thus Julian's image of the deity. Her Mother Jesus should not be seen, however, as a simple enlargement or projection of the usual and actual medieval mother onto a heavenly screen. Although her description indicates that some women of her time must indeed have demonstrated the behavior she lauds, what is more important is the acceptance of the female self inherent in the image and the power, plenitude, love, and worship in the sense of profound respect it accords to women. Important, too, is the longing the image expresses for the acknowledgement or restoration of the tie between mother and daughter, the umbilicus, as it were, of the divine scheme.

NOTES

1. Francine du Plessix Gray discusses the notion of female friendship in a review of Nina Auerbach's *Communities of Women: An Idea in Fiction*, the *New York Times Book Review* 19 June 1978. Mrs Belmont is credited with this remark by Ashley Montague, *The Natural Superiority of Women* (New York: Collier Books, 1968), p. 122.

2. *See* Virginia Woolf's *A Room of One's Own* (New York: Harcourt, Brace, 1963).

3. From the Francine du Plessix Gray review; *see* note 1.

4. *See* Gray, note 1.

5. On the subordination of Mary in the heavenly hierarchy *see* Sister Mary Gripkey, *The Blessed Virgin Mary as Mediatrix in the Latin and Old French Legends Prior to the Fourteenth Century* (Washington, D.C.: The Catholic University of America, 1938).

6. For discussion of the differences between French or Norman French culture and that of the South *see* Ford Maddox Ford, *Provence* (New York: The Ecco Press, 1979).

7. *See* Heata Dillard on "Women in Reconquest Castile" in *Women in Medieval Society*, ed. Susan Mosher Stuard (University of Pennsylvania Press, 1976), pp. 71–94.

8. *See* Frances and Joseph Gies, *Women in the Middle Ages* (New York: Thomas Crowell, 1978), pp. 42–6.

9. *See* G. Rattray Taylor, "Medieval Sexual Behaviour" and "Medieval Sexual Ideal" in *Sex in History* (New York: Harper and Row, 1970), pp. 19–71.

10. *See* the living arrangements of Pandarus described by Chaucer in *Troilus and Criseyde*, for example, or the scene in the bedchamber of Bercilak's castle in *Sir Gawain and the Green Knight*. Frances and Joseph Gies have also attempted to describe *Life in a Medieval Castle* New York: Thomas Y. Crowell, 1974), but their work is too general to be truly helpful.

11. According to Taylor, *Sex in History*, p. 97, in "the earliest Celtic versions" of the Tristan legend, the "drama comes from the fact that he has killed the husband of Brangwen, a sorceress, who is determined to revenge herself. But in the medieval versions, Brangwen recedes into the background." Thus, the evolution of Brangwen as lady-in-waiting might be a fascinating subject for psychological investigation.

12. All quotations from Beroul's *Tristan and Iseult* are from the translation of Janet Hillier Caulkins and Guy R. Mermier (Paris: Librairie A. Champion, 1967); *see* p. 21, 11. 339–43.

13. Ibid., p. 21, 11. 345–50.

14. Ibid., p. 22, 1. 369 and 11. 370–1.

15. Ibid., p. 22, 11. 372–80.

16. In Beroul's version, this episode is mentioned but not dramatized.

17. Ibid., p. 28, 11. 511–18.

18. Ibid., pp. 28–9, 11. 529–34.

19. *See Cligès* in *Arthurian Romances*, trans. W. W. Confort (London: Dent, 1968), pp. 161–2.

20. Ibid., p. 169.

21. *Floris and Blancheflour* is French in origin but was translated—and changed considerably—in the thirteenth century.

22. I cite the edition of E. B. Taylor, *Floris and Blancheflour*, throughout (Oxford: Clarendon Press, 1927); *see* p. 30, 11. 35–51.

23. Ibid., pp. 30–1, 11. 55–62.

24. Ibid., p. 31, 11. 75–9.

25. Ibid., p. 33, 11. 134–41.

26. Ibid., p. 33, 11. 142–52.

27. Ibid., p. 38, 11. 313–20.

28. *See also* Chaucer's "The Man of Law's Tale" and *Aucassin and Nicolette*, the anonymous chant-fable.

29. E. B. Taylor, p. 55, 11. 883–8.

30. Ibid., p. 57, 11. 944–9.

31. Ibid., p. 57, 11. 951–6.

32. Ibid., p. 59, 11. 995–1018.

33. F. N. Robinson, *The Works of Geoffrey Chaucer* (Cambridge, Mass: Houghton-Mifflin, 1957), p. 498, 11. 798–801.

34. O. S. Pickering, ed., *The South English Nativity of Mary and Christ* (Heidelberg: Carl Winter, 1975), p. 72. Anne is not with Mary here.

35. A. Franklin., ed., *Seven Miracle Plays* (Oxford: Oxford University Press, 1963), p. 139.

36. Ibid., p. 45.

37. *See* Sigmund Freud, *Jokes and Their Relation to the Unconscious* (New York: W. W. Norton, 1963), pp. 233–5.

38. Translated into English as *From Camelot to Joyous Guard* by J. Neale Carman (Lawrence, Kansas: University of Kansas Press, 1974), p. 143.

39. Ibid., p. 143.

40. Ibid., pp. 143–4.

41. Ibid., p. 144.

42. Ibid.

43. Ibid.

44. Ibid.

45. *See* Sybylle Harkson, *Women in the Middle Ages* (New York: Abner Schram, 1975), pp. 29–33.

46. Ibid., p. 30.

47. Ibid., pp. 30–1.

48. Ibid., pp. 29–33.

49. On the *frauenfrage*, the woman question, see Brenda M. Bolton, "Mulieres Sanctae," in *Women in Medieval Society*, pp. 141–58.

50. In the *Historia Ecclesiastica*.

51. Sister Mary of the Incarnation Byrne, *The Tradition of the Nun in Medieval England* (Washington, D.C.: Catholic University of America Press, 1932), pp. 74–5.

52. Ibid., pp. 74–5, note.

53. The basic unit of social organization having been the *comitatus*, the fine gradations of later feudal hierarchy were not present. *See* chapter 3.

54. C. Horstmann, ed., *The Lives of Women Saints of Our Countrie of England* (London: E.E.T.S., 1886), p. vi.

55. Ibid., p. xviii, presents evidence of the author's Catholicism.

56. Ibid., pp. 11–2.

57. Ibid., pp. 12–3.

58. Ibid., p. 13.

59. *See* chapter 2.

60. *See* chapters 2 and 3. Active religious women frequently reject their natural mothers in the literature.

61. Horstmann, *The Lives of Women Saints*, p. 54.

62. Ibid.

63. Ibid.

64. Ibid., p. 55.

65. Ibid., p. 59.

66. Ibid., p. 59.

67. Ibid., p. 196; *see* this Life in its entirety, pp. 189–213, for the mother-daughter relationship depicted in it.

68. Ibid., p. 52.

69. Ibid.

70. Ibid.

71. Ibid., pp. 52-3.

72. Ibid., p. 53.

73. I refer to the F. N. Robinson edition of *The Works of Geoffrey Chaucer* (Cambridge, Mass.: Houghton-Miflin, 1957); *see* p. 161, 11. 461-2.

74. Ibid., p. 161, 1. 467.

75. Ibid., p. 161, 1. 484.

76. I refer here to the Prioress giving her dogs white bread, for example, in a time of famine and to her easy pity, as depicted in the General Prologue.

77. *Works of Chaucer*, pp. 161-3, 1. 510, 1. 543, 1. 619, and 1. 656 respectively.

78. Ibid., p. 162, 1. 593.

79. *See* Beverly Boyd, ed., *The Middle English Miracles of the Virgin* (San Marino, Cal.: Huntington Library, 1964), pp. 30-49.

80. This tale in verse, printed by Boyd, dates from the twelfth century and is an analogue of Chaucer's "The Man of Law's Tale."

81. Boyd, *The Middle English Miracles of the Virgin*, p. 65.

82. Ibid.

83. Ibid.

84. Ibid., p. 66.

85. Ibid., pp. 66-7.

86. *See* Johannes Herolt, *Miracles of the Blessed Virgin Mary*, trans. C. C. Swinton Bland (London: Routledge, 1928).

87. *See* Deutsch, *The Psychology of Women* (1944; paperback ed., New York: Bantam Books, 1973), p. 240.

88. As R.E.L. Masters notes in *Eros and Evil* (Baltimore: Penguin, 1974), pp. 169ff.

89. Another example, as in Herolt, of humanizing the Virgin.

90. *The Blessed Virgin Mary as Mediatrix in the Latin and Old French Legends Prior to the Fourteenth Century* (Washington, D.C.: The Catholic University of America, 1938), p. 219.

91. I refer to the edition of William Patterson Cumming (London: E.E.T.S., 1929), p. 101.

92. *St. Birgitta*, pp. 100-1.

93. A full-length study by Robert Karl Stone, *Middle English Prose Style: Margery Kempe and Julian of Norwich* (The Hague: Mouton, 1970), although quite illuminating in other ways, and careful, does not take this evolution of mothering from figure of speech into a religious symbol into account.

94. Quotations are from the edition and translation of Dom Roger Hudleston O.S.B. (London: Burns Oates, 1952); *see* p. 8.

95. Ibid.

96. Ibid., pp. 11–12.

97. Ibid., p. 46.

98. Ibid.

99. Ibid., p. 110.

100. Ibid., p. 120.

101. Ibid., p. 121.

102. Ibid., p. 123.

103. Ibid.

104. Ibid., p. 124.

105. Ibid., p. 125.

EVE'S ORPHANS

"It is a fragmentary tragedy
Within the universal whole. . . ."
—*Wallace Stevens*[1]

If the mother-daughter bond seems to have been the model in literature at least for relationships between and among medieval women, the question remains as to the origins of the notion that women have been and are rivals and enemies to each other. Does the latter image exist in medieval literature, and if so, in which works and for what ends?

It seems doubtful whether women's rivalry was ever as virulent as the popular imagination would have it. A fair amount of projection appears to have been involved. As Ashley Montague puts it,

> Vendettas and internecine conflicts are essentially masculine activities, and the most pathological form that such activities take, namely, war, is exclusively a masculine invention and ghastliness.[2]

Women's rivalry, that is, tends to look pale when compared with the Hundred Years War, the slaughter of the Albigensians, or World War II. The attribution of a particular kind of intolerance to women presupposes that the same values and identifications that prevail in the Star Chamber or corporate boardroom will prevail in the nursery.[3]

It has been pointed out that the "Middle Ages were the last period in which women enjoyed lives that were nearly parallel to those of men."[4] While this is in some ways a most misleading statement—given, for example, the inequity of the adultery laws and the predominance of men in positions of power both secular and ecclesiastical, the parallelism breaks down—one does come away from portraits of medieval women together feeling that the scheming, distrustful, plotting woman, the woman set against other women, is a rarity. The argument of Mahl and Koon

In *The Female Spectator* suggests a greater sense of community among women; they write of the nuns in early convents working in the scriptoria, and the participation of women in commerce and in guild industry.[5] But these are women who to some extent existed independently or who, like the peasant women, were needed for their labor. Perhaps also women, even if exploited, were better able to see themselves as an exploited group rather than as individuals failing or succeeding on the strength of their sexual allure, but such a question is beyond the scope of this book.

Depictions of rivalry among woman and/or the complete isolation of one woman and her subsequent dependency upon a man are to be found in English literature of the medieval period in works that treat of male rivalry in the form of war and have, moreover, as a good part of their thematic concern the point of view out of which a warrior ethic evolves. There is in these works a conflict, overt or subliminal, between the courtly ethos and the warrior ethos, between a mother-identified culture and a father-identified one. The father-identified, or *patrist*, point of view, with its values of prowess, competition, and male fellowship, represents women as betrayers, both toward men and toward each other.[6]

The patrist point of view is clear in the writing of Sir Thomas Malory. His Guenever is positively allied with no woman. Instead she is threatened by and pitted against Morgan le Fay. In contrast to Brangain, for example, in the *Tristan and Iseult* legend, Morgan and the women of her court are intent upon depriving Guenever of her sole protector, Launcelot.[7] In this scene from *Le Morte d'Arthur*, for example, four queens find Launcelot sleeping:

> anon as these queens looked on his face, they knew it was Sir Launcelot. Then they began for to strive for that knight, every each one said they would have him to her love.
> "We shall not strive," said Morgan le Fay, that was King Arthur's sister. "I shall put an enchantment upon him that he shall not awake in six hours, and then I will lead him away unto my castle, and when he is surely within my hold, I shall take the enchantment from him, and then let him choose which of us he will have unto paramour."[8]

The spell is cast, but by the time a damsel brings Launcelot his supper, the enchantment has worn off. He complains that he does not know how he has come to the castle, and she promises to enlighten him if he proves to be the knight he is reputed to be, by the next day:

And on the morn early came these four queens, passingly well beseen, they bidding him good morn and he them again.

"Sir knight," the four queens said, "thou must understand that thou art our prisoner, and we know well that thou art Sir Launcelot du Lake, King Ban's son, and because we understand your worthiness, that thou art the noblest knight living, and as we know well there can no lady have thy love but one, and that is Queen Guenever, and now thou shalt lose her for ever, and she thee, and therefore thee behoveth now to choose one of us four."[9]

Morgan moves forward to reiterate:

"I am Queen Morgan le Fay, queen of the land of Gore, and here is the Queen of Northgales, and the Queen of Eastland, and the Queen of the Out Isles; now choose one of us which thou wilt have to thy paramour, for thou mayest not choose or else in this prison to die."[10]

Launcelot utterly rejects their advances, of course:

"This is a hard case," said Sir Launcelot, "that either I must die or else choose one of you, yet had I lever to die in this prison with worship, than to have one of you to my paramour maugre my head. And therefore ye be answered, I will none of you, for ye be false enchantresses, and as for my lady, Dame Guenever, were I at my liberty as I was, I would prove it on you or on yours, that she is the truest lady unto her lord living."[11]

Malory has not only presented these women's jealousy of Guenever but also depicted their duplicity and cunning as a kind of pack. These women have banded together not for any friendly purpose—and certainly not from that friendship and troth with which Malory sees his Knights of the Round Table uniting—but in order to enchant and entrap a man. Moreover, Launcelot, the near-perfect and true, is delivered from his predicament by his breakfast damsel. In this work, he can be saved only if the woman at the same time betrays her own kind:

Right so at the noon came the damosel unto him with his dinner, and asked him what cheer.

"Truly, fair damsel," said Sir Launcelot, "in my life days never so ill."

"Sir," she said, "that me repentest, but and ye will be ruled by me, I shall help you out of this distress, and ye shall have no shame nor villainy, so that ye hold me a promise."

"Fair damosel, I will grant you, and sore I am of these queens sorceresses afeared, for they have destroyed many a good knight."

"Sir," said she, "that is sooth, and for the renown and bounty that they hear of you they would have your love, and sir, they say, your name is Sir Launcelot du Lake, the flower of knights, and they be passing wroth with you that ye have refused them. But sir, and ye would promise to help me to help my father on Tuesday next coming, that hath made a tournament betwixt him and the King of Northgales, for the last Tuesday past my father lost the field through three knights of Arthur's court, and ye will be there on Tuesday next coming, and help my father, to-morn or prime, by the grace of God, I shall deliver you clean."[12]

Malory celebrates a male-centered and father-identified culture, a culture of war and strife. His heroes are the heroes of epic, of *Le Chanson de Roland*, rather than those of the South of France and the Courts of Love. Maurice Valency writes of the ladies in the *chanson de geste* that "in spite of the summary treatment they ordinarily receive," they "serve their knights indefatigably."

> The epic knight, like his modern counterpart, the cowboy of fiction, was more interested in deeds than in women. . . love was the natural tribute which the female paid to the dazzling male, who, for his part, was accustomed to receive it with the carelessness of one who had no present need.[13]

Valency penetrates to the fantasy at the core of this literary convention: the heroes in work of this kind are admired as warriors.

> The usual rationalization is that in the unsettled times when these stories were written, the paramount need of a lady was for a man who could protect her, so that the indispensable attribute of the hero of the romance would be prowess. Perhaps this conclusion bears some relation to the fact but the relation to the fantasy is more apparent. Women in our day stand in little need of the sort of protection which the knightly champion could afford them; they have the police. Yet the fictional qualifications of the romantic lover have not changed essentially since the time of the crusades. The audience for which the *chansons de geste* were designed was not much interested in the intellectual attributes of the epic hero. Intellect was an attribute of traitors and wizards. Love was for mollycoddles. The epic knight was a man among men.[14]

A fantasy of this kind cannot admit of women being independent or strong or motherly and nurturing. Its implication for the perception of female behavior is that a woman will be ready and willing to do anything, including betraying mere women friends, in order to secure the protection of a man, as the damosel is perfectly willing to betray her mistress and the women of her mistress' court in exchange for Launcelot's prowess.

Just as Morgan attempts to rob Guenever of Launcelot, Guenever attempts to keep Launcelot from another later in the work. Dame Elaine, the mother of Galahad, appears at Guenever's court. Both Elaine and Guenever wish to capture Launcelot for the night.

> So when Elaine was brought unto Queen Guenever either made other good cheer by countenance, but nothing with hearts. But all men and women spake of the beauty of Dame Elaine, and of her great riches.
>
> Then at night the queen commanded that Dame Elaine should sleep in a chamber nigh her chamber, and all under one roof; and so it was done as the queen commanded. Then the queen sent for Sir Launcelot and bad him come to her chamber that night: "Or else I am sure," said the queen, "that ye will go to your lady's bed, Dame Elaine, by whom ye gat Galahad."
>
> "Ah, madam," said Sir Launcelot, "never say ye so, for that I did was against my will."
>
> "Then," said the queen, "look that ye come to me when I send for you."[15]

Dame Elaine is not to be outdone by this, however; she sends her lady-in-waiting to fetch Launcelot so that by the time Guenever's lady-in-waiting arrives at his bed it is cold. Moreover, he "clatters" in his sleep of Guenever who, hearing him, banishes him. This is not the end of the quarrel between the two women. Elaine, after Guenever has rebuked Launcelot, rebukes the queen:

> "Madam, ye are greatly to blame for Sir Launcelot, for now ye have lost him, for I saw and heard by his countenance that he is mad forever. Alas, madam, ye do great sin, and to yourself great dishonor, for ye have a land of your own, and therefore it is your part to love him: for there is no queen in this world hath such another king as ye have. And if ye were not I might have the love of my lord Sir Launcelot; and cause I have to love him for he had my maidenhood, and by him I have borne a fair son, and his name is Galahad, and he shall be in his time the best night in the world."[16]

Not only is this harsh and possessive but also taunting in that Dame Elaine, in the mode of the male-centered or phallic mother, boasts about her son to Guenever.[17] The queen responds by forbidding Elaine the court:

> "Dame Elaine," said the queen, "when it is daylight I charge you and command you to avoid my court; and for the love you owe unto Sir Launcelot discover not his counsel, for and ye do, it will be his death."[18]

Not even their realization that both have lost Launcelot unites them. Dame Elaine remarks that neither of the two women will be likely to "rejoice him," but this does not arrest her banishment:

> "Alas," said fair Elaine, and "Alas," said Queen Guenever, "for now I wot well we have lost him for ever."
> So on the morn Dame Elaine took her leave to depart, and she would not longer abide.[19]

It is at last King Arthur who protects Elaine, bringing her "on her way with more than an hundred knights through a forest," for women, in Malory, cannot nurture or protect each other.[20]

A possessive rivalry between women also appears in Walter Map's narrative "On the Comradeship of Sadius and Galo." In this story with its "mingled themes of woman's jealousy and man's friendship," the twelfth-century courtier has borrowed amply from the misogynistic tradition of the classical world.[21] Two friends, "equal in character, youth and comeliness, well learned in the science of arms. . . loved each other with warm and honourable affection in which they stood proved amid adversity."[22] Galo has a problem, however: the queen of the country in which he lives is passionately in love with him. "No form of, solicitation did the queen leave untried, no form of persuasion; completely did she show herself a bawd by her immodesty, and whatever passion is wont to urge to the love-crazed, this she attempted."[23] Galo, although polite to the queen, wishes to guard the "camp of his chastity" against her advances and turns away her gifts, not knowing any other means by which to discourage her.[24] His comrade Sadius comes to the rescue, and tells the queen that Galo cannot comply with her desires since "he is sexless," that is, physically lacking. The queen, incredulous, sends her maid to find out the truth, instructing her "to approach Galo so that she could slip into his embrace, and bade her cling closely to him, when both were slightly clad, and put her hand upon his privy parts, and to report, without yielding her won honour, whether he could or could not."[25] As soon as she sends the maid, she "straightway repenteth of her sending."[26] A long lament follows, and an interrogation of another woman-in-waiting as to how the maiden she has sent was dressed.[27] The second woman, too, is not above telling tales on the first.

> No need to complain of her for having left behind gold, fine garments, or any aids of that sort; she paid regard to all things, but gave no thought to a quick return." The Queen: "And I thought her such a simpleton, such a fool in all these wiles." Lais: "She a simpleton! O, how very clever in the matter of a certain gentleman, if it were only right for me to tell!" The Queen: "Kind Lais mine, tell me all." Lais: "She is making a set at Galo with all the means in her power."[28]

Ero, the first woman, eventually returns. The Queen questions her closely, as Ero tries to be politic in her replies:

> The Queen: "What took place?" Ero: "I came, I touched, but I was repulsed. And yet I doubt not of his power." The Queen: "Why didst thou not return at once? What pleasure foundst thou in delay?" Ero: "Desire feeleth delay in the shortest moment. I left here just now and hastened with all my might: how could I have come more quickly?" The Queen: From the time I sent thee on my errand till now, thou couldst have returned from a journey of ten miles, but thou wert unwilling to go forth unless well arrayed. Wert thou going to be married?" Ero: "It was well to have the power to win his favour until I could know: and I almost won his favour, and I felt that the man was sound and ready, had he felt you; but when he realized it was an inferior, one less fit and far less suitable than yourself, he cast me out."[29]

The Queen at this continent reply flares with jealous and, needless to say, irrational anger:

> The Queen: "Now I know that thou art a wanton in thy love," and seizing her by the hair she threw her on the floor, struck her with hands and feet, and gave her almost lifeless to her companions to guard most carefully, that no liberty be allowed her. She then went off to her room, cast herself upon her bed, and uttered all that baneful love can teach dark hearts. . . .[30]

A relationship between women of this kind, based on rivalry, furious and bootless jealousy, and an irrational desire for an unattainable male, must be drawn once the elements of a patrist viewpoint are given.[31] In Walter Map's tale, all these elements are present: the close bonds between the two men, the emphasis on their prowess as warriors, their indifference to the woman, Galo's concern for his own chastity, and the necessary projection of sexual desire onto the woman.[32] No other relationship can be conceived of between women in works of this sort, from the *chansons de geste* to the American Westerns.

The conflict between the warrior ethic and the courtly ethic did not remain subliminal in the medieval period, of course. It finds its most explicit expression and resolution in the works of such troubadours as Guillaume IX. The greatest English work that deals, if obliquely, with the opposition of the love of war and the war of love as well as the codes that give rise to both is Chaucer's *Troilus and Criseyde*.

One does not and cannot attempt to treat of the entire conflict in this immense and complex work. A question more proper for this study is why Chaucer has isolated Criseyde from the women who enter the poem, that is, why he has orphaned her so completely. However, it must be pointed out here, because of the greater implications of that utter orphaning, that the tragedy of the lovers is not only or merely set against the backdrop of the Trojan War but is in certain ways the result of the war and the attitudes that instigated it and perpetuate it in the poem. As George D. Economou writes, in an excellent article on "The Two Venuses and Courtly Love,"

> That the history of Troilus and Criseyde is closely related to the history of Troy has been widely recognized for some time. The poem opens at a time when the city's defenses are enjoying unqualified success in holding the Greek threat in check—even though the seeds of Troy's destruction have already been sown by the defection of Criseyde's father, Calkas the priest. . . . During this period, Troilus emerges as one of Troy's most formidable champions. His effectiveness as a warrior increases as he takes on "Loves heigh servise" and reaches its highest point with his fulfillment as a lover, a development fully in keeping with the courtly tradition of the lover's private and public lives coming together.[33]

Troilus, then, becomes the courtly lover *par excellence.* He is thus the younger brother in a figurative sense, too, of Trojan heroes such as

Hector, his actual brother, and of the heroes of the Greek code such as Diomed, who stands not so much for brutality as for the warrior-ethic that eventually destroys the lovers and the Trojan civilization. Both Troilus and Criseyde attempt to live in accordance with another set of mores, those Taylor would call *matrist*.[34] Both are forced back into the authoritarian world of politics, power play, and war. Economou writes that

> a single event undoes the love and eventually the city. The decision of the Trojan parliament to exchange Criseyde for Antenor destroys both the security of lovers and city.[35]

The events that follow upon this action, I would add, symbolize the defeat of the courtly code itself, which was in turn predicated upon love and trust between men and women, with the woman taking up—psychologically—the mothering role.[36]

Criseyde is to a great extent depicted as a woman caught between two codes, the courtly code with its admission of women to equality and mothering strength—and therefore its allowance of female friendships as in Chrétien's courtly *Cligès*—and the heroic code that as in Malory and Map forces women into subordinate and dependent roles in which the male is seen as protector.[37] One of Criseyde's salient characteristics is, of course, her fear, or her fearfulness. She has reason to be afraid: from Book I, she is presented as literally orphaned, her mother dead and her traitorous father having abandoned her. In a position of extreme vulnerability in a city at war, she is a widow, in the emotional guardianship of a rather slippery uncle, Pandarus, and living a life as cloistered and enclosed as possible in her house and among her women. As she tells Pandarus, "I am of Grekes so fered that I deye."[38] She is also, as she should be, afraid of letting herself trust the promises of men: " 'Men make love to women whether they will or not,' she muses, 'and when they want no more of them, they let them down.' "[39] However, even with all her fearfulness, and her remarks on this subject are too numerous to mention,[40] she attempts to become the strong and supportive courtly woman: "I am my own woman, well at ease," she declares at one point. Once Troilus has assured her of her sovereignty in the relationship, she is capable of comforting him, arranging meetings, and, until the fatal trade, governing her life.[41]

What are the other women like in this work? Behind all of them, there is the image of Helen, to whom I return at another point. Chaucer presents the women who come to visit Criseyde as the dupes and playthings of a warrior culture to whom and in whom she can neither trust nor confide:

> But as one sees all about town
> It was the custom for women to visit their friends,
> So a group of women came to see Criseyde,
> In compassionate cheerfulness, intending
> To delight her with their tales, which would be
> Dear enough at half a penny; these townswomen
> Sat themselves down, and I'll tell you what they said.
>
> Said the first one, "I am truely glad
> For you that you will be able to see your father
> Again." Another said, "I'm not glad—
> She's been with us too little as it is."
> And the third said, "I hope that she
> Will bring peace on both sides—
> May God guide her when she goes!"
> These words and these womanish concerns
> She heard as little as if she were not there;
> For, God knows, her heart is in other matters,
> Although her body sat among them there;
> Her attention was somewhere else;
> Her soul followed Troilus—
> Without speaking, she always thought of him.[42]

Although the women try to lessen her discomfort with their chatter, either they have no conception of the gravity of the situation, or they pretend not to know the real danger that attends Criseyde:

> These women who thought to please her
> Began to chatter away about nothing.
> But such vanity could not ease her,
> For she, all the meanwhile, burned
> With a passion other than they knew,
> So that she felt her heart almost give way
> For grief and in weariness of their company.[43]

When tears rise to her eyes and she sighs heavily, thinking about the loss of Troilus, the women misinterpret:

> And those fools who sat about
> Thought that she wept and sighed so deeply
> Because she was about to take leave of them,
> And never amuse herself with them any more.
> And those who had known her a long time
> Observed her weeping, and thought it
> Fellow-feeling; and each of them wept for her distress.
>
> And busily they began to comfort her
> About things she was thinking, God knows,
> Little enough about; and they tried to distract her
> With stories, and begged her to cheer up.
> But the kind of comfort they gave her
> Was such as a man with a headache would feel
> If someone were to scratch him on his heel![44]

Criseyde cannot confide in these women because their world is the world of "playe" and "disport," certainly very far from the *realpolitik* of the situation in Troy. They do not realize the danger she is in, nor do they realize the implications of the trade. One of the women is even unrealistic enough to hope that the bartering of Criseyde may bring about a peace when it is precisely the treatment of a woman as a piece of property that has brought about the entire war.[45] Peripheral and childish in the world of power and political expediency, these women cannot even face reality: cold comfort for Criseyde indeed.

Criseyde reverts to type, as it were, as the society abandons its principles of justice and respect for persons in the parliament scene. " 'She is no prisoner,' " Hector declares, " '. . . It is not our custom to sell women here,' " but the crowd, frightened out of its wits and out of its human values, does just that. The people of Troy are willing to sell a free woman in order to retrieve their best warrior, or the man they think will serve them best in wartime but who eventually betrays his city also. It is significant that the motherless Criseyde is returned to her treacherous father again and significant that Chaucer has Calkas claim his daughter as the only piece of property he has left. He tells the Greeks:

> "So I left all my possessions and came to you,
> Thinking in this way, lords, to please you.
> I wasn't bothered by that loss,
> I swear truely, and I would be perfectly happy
> For you to use anything I still have in Troy.
>
> "Except a daughter that I left, alas!
> Sleeping at home, when I started out from Troy."[46]

While Calkas tells the Greeks of his lost "tresor,"[47] Criseyde wails:

> "Oh, Calkas, father, all the blame is yours!
> Oh, my mother, called by the name Argyve,
> Woe to the day on which you gave me life!"[48]

Criseyde, betrayed by her father as the culture of love in this work is betrayed by the culture of war, turns in the all-male world of the Greek camp from the courtly Troilus and towards the powerful Diomed. Isolated and dependent upon a male for protection, she becomes like the women in the *chansons de geste* and like those in contemporary fantasy of whom Valency writes, who must be alienated from other women.[49] Criseyde's return to this primitive status is correlative to that of Helen, the woman-as-possession who, moreover, feels at ease in that role. It signifies the failure of the courtly code and the ascendancy of, or regression to, the warrior ethic that must orphan women and men both in more ways than one.

The delineation of female characters has as much to do with the attitude of the authors as with anything else, of course. Those who, like Malory and Map, subscribed to the patrist view of men were severely limited in their delineation of women. As lesser geniuses, they, Malory and Map, created works that, in this respect at least, reflect their state of mind rather than the symbolic truth of the human condition. Chaucer, on the other hand, has given expression to a state of mind formed in part by a culture that, just as it deprived women of their mothers, as frequently led men to deny the courtly, loving, and mother-identified part of themselves.

So, from remarking the absence of mothers and importance of fathers, one returns to the absence of mothers and presence of fathers again. However, we have seen how, even in the works of a strongly father-identified period, surrogate mothers appear to nurture and teach when the natural mother-daughter bond is depicted as much weakened; how women, portrayed in the poetry for the most part without their natural mothers, seem to take a motherly and supportive attitude towards each other; how, in the imaginings of male and female writers, heavenly mothers exist upon whom the women in these works may model themselves. We have seen a true courtly ethos giving birth to positive images of women old and young. Although works dictated by the warrior ethic depict relationships between women as vicious and competitive, we have seen the mother-daughter bond manifesting itself in the works of a culture that discouraged the formation and maintenance of that bond.

How far these investigations take us into medieval life I do not know. I have attempted to penetrate attitudes, to describe how men and women saw the mother-daughter relationship, and to chronicle or analyze symbolic events in a collective psyche. I have tried to avoid facile deductions about day-to-day living based on the imaginative work of primarily male poets and writers. The historians will have to do much more work among the records for that. I do think that one thing becomes clear in the literature, however, and that is the basic strength of the mother-daughter bond, as even men subconsciously opposed to it and afraid of it perceived it. How great the impulse to rescue, save, protect, nurture, and teach our own kind must be if the effort of so many years to make us ashamed of the wombs we came from did not obliterate first needs and first loyalties.

If women in later centuries were seen as or became less nurturing to each other and more male-centered, if they forgot, or let themselves be trained to forget, the innocence of Mother Eve and their own orphaning, then this has been, as I believe Chaucer shows, a general and very human loss indeed.

NOTES

1. Wallace Stevens, "Esthetique du Mal" *Poems* (New York: Random House, 1929), p. 123.

2. Ashley Montague, *The Natural Superiority of Women* (New York: Collier Books, 1974), p. 34.

3. *See* Phyllis Chesler, *About Men* (New York: Simon and Schuster, 1978), pp. 234-49 especially.

4. *The Female Spectator*, ed. Mahl and Koon (Bloomington, Indiana: Indiana University Press, 1977), p. 5.

5. Ibid., p. 5.

6. *See* G. Rattray Taylor's important—and ignored—work, *Sex in History* (New York: Harper and Row, 1970), pp. 72–108.

7. On the relationship of Brangain and Iseult, *see* chapter 5.

8. I cite the edition of Janet Cowan (Middlesex, England: Penguin Books, 1969) throughout; *see* vol.1, pp. 197–8. Malory's *Le Morte D'Arthur*, of the fifteenth century, is not to be confused with the Old French prose work *La Mort le Roi Artu* discussed in chapter 5.

9. Ibid., vol. 1, p. 198.

10. Ibid., vol. 1, pp. 198–9.

11. Ibid., vol. 1, p. 199.

12. Ibid., vol. 1, pp. 199–200.

13. Maurice Valency, *In Praise of Love* (New York: Farrar, Straus and Giroux, 1975), pp. 54–5.

14. Ibid., p. 55.

15. Malory, *Le Morte D'Arthur*, vol. 2, p. 200.

16. Ibid., vol. 2, p. 202.

17. This is the classic case of mothers being honored in patrist society in the bearing of male offspring; *see* Chesler, *About Men*, p. 32, for example.

18. Malory, *Le Morte D'Arthur*, vol. 2, p. 203.

19. Ibid.

20. Ibid.

21. *See* the translation by Frederick Tupper and Marbury Bladen Ogle of Walter Map, *De Nugis Curialium* (*Courtier's Trifles*) (New York: Macmillan, 1924), p. xviii; the entire tale is included by Tupper and Ogle, whom I cite hereafter; see pp. 131–55.

22. Ibid., p. 131.

23. Ibid., pp. 131–2.

24. Ibid., p. 132.

25. Ibid., p. 134.

26. Ibid.

27. Ibid., pp. 134–7.

28. Ibid., p. 137.

29. Ibid., pp. 137–8.

30. Ibid., p. 138.

31. Ibid.

32. Taylor, *Sex in History*, pp. 80–5; according to Taylor, the father-identified personality sees the mother as a betrayer and inclines to those activities the culture considers "masculine"; he would be drawn into all-male environments that, while satisfying latent homoerotic tendencies, would reenforce the "masculine" identification. According to Taylor, this personality type would tend to author-

itarianism, rigidity, intolerance, and the like, its only "advantage" being a kind of energy (generally destructive) from repressed instincts and drives.

33. George D. Economou, "The Two Venuses and Courtly Love," in *In Pursuit of Perfection*, ed. Joan M. Ferrante and George D. Economou (Port Washington, N.Y., and London: Kennikat Press, 1975), pp. 17–50; p. 40.

34. *See* Taylor, *Sex in History* pp. 80–5; Taylor connects the mother-identified personality, with its sexual, political, and religious tolerance, its concern for welfare instead of chastity, and its artistic and intellectual openness with the culture of Provence and the development there of the courtly love codes and the Albigensian movement.

35. Economou, "The Two Venuses," pp. 40–1.

36. Valency, *In Praise of Love*, pp. 32–3.

37. *See* W. W. Comfort, trans., *Cligès* in *Arthurian Romances* (London: Dent, 1968), pp. 91–179. *See also* chapter 5.

38. *The Works of Geoffrey Chaucer*, ed. F. N. Robinson (Cambridge, Mass.: Houghton-Mifflin, 1957), p. 403, 1. 124.

39. *Works of Chaucer*, p. 409, 11. 734–5: "Men loven wommen al biside hire leve; / And whan hem leste namore, lat hem byleve!"

40. *See*, for example, Book 2, 11. 113–30; Book 2, 1. 309 ff.; Book 2, 1. 455 ff. especially.

41. *Works of Chaucer*, p. 409, 1. 750ff.

42. *Works of Chaucer*, p. 448, 11. 680-700:

> But as men seen in towne, and al aboute,
> That wommen usen frendes to visite,
> So to Criseyde of wommen com a route,
> For pitous joie, and wenden hire delite;
> And with hire tales, deere ynough a myte,
> Thise wommen, which that in the cite dwelle,
> They sette hem down, and seyde as I shall telle.
>
> Quod first that oon, "I am glad, trewely,
> Bycause of yow, that shal youre fader see."
> Another seyde, "Ywis, so nam nat I;
> For al to litel hath she with us be."
> Quod tho the thridde, "I hope, ywis, that she
> Shall bryngen us the pees on every syde,
> That, whan she goth, almyghty God hire gide!"
>
> Tho wordes and tho wommanysshe thynges,
> She herde hem right as though she thennes were;

> For, God it woot, hire herte on othir thyng is.
> Although the body sat among hem there,
> Hire advertence is alwey elleswhere;
> For Troilus ful faste hire soule soughte;
> Withouten word, on hym alwey she thoughte.

43. *Works of Chaucer*, p. 448, ll. 701-7:

> Thise wommen, that thus wenden hire to plese,
> Aboute naught gonne alle hire tales spende.
> Swich vanyte ne kan don hire non ese,
> As she that al this mene while brende
> Of other passioun than that they wende,
> So that she felte almost hire herte dye
> For wo and wery of that compaignie.

44. *Works of Chaucer*, p. 448, ll. 715-28:

> And thilke fooles sittynge hire aboute
> Wenden that she wepte and siked sore
> Bycause that she sholde out of that route
> Departe, and nevere pleye with hem more.
> And they that had yknowen hire of yore
> Seigh hire so wepe, and thoughte it kyndenesse,
> And ech of hem wepte eke for hire destresse.
>
> And bisyly they gonnen hire comforten
> Of thyng, God woot, on which she litel thoughte;
> And with hire tales wenden hire disporten,
> And to be glad they often hire bysoughte.
> But swich an ese therwith they hire wroughte,
> Right as a man is esed for to feele,
> For ache of hed, to clawen hym on his heele!

45. *See* Book 2, l. 1555 ff.; Eleyne is perfectly at ease in the warriors' company. She, too, like the visiting women, is perfectly able to "pleye" (l. 1668) as she is, indeed, the plaything of men.

46. *Works of Chaucer*, p. 442, ll. 87-93:

> "Thus al my good I lefte and to yow wente,
> Wenyng in this yow, lordes, for to plese.
> But al that los ne doth me no disese.

I vouchesauf, as wisly have I joie,
For yow to lese al that I have in Troie,

Save of a doughter that I lefte, allas!
Slepyng at hom, whanne out of Troie I sterte."

47. *Works of Chaucer*, p. 441, 1. 85.
48. *Works of Chaucer*, p. 449, 11. 761–3:

"O Calkas, fader, thyn be al this synne!
O moder myn, that cleped were Argyve,
Wo worth that day that thow me bere on lyve!"

49. Valency, *In Praise of Love*, pp. 54–5.

BIBLIOGRAPHICAL NOTES

The reference notes at the end of each chapter contain the sources drawn upon in the writing of this book. As it would be pointless to reprint all of them here, the following information will, I hope, be helpful to the reader who is interested in pursuing a particular subject further or who is interested in the ideational or cultural background of the analyses in this work. In this hope, I have sorted the references into the topics of medieval poetry and prose, philosophy and the history of ideas, and women's studies, psychology, and literary criticism.

MEDIEVAL POETRY AND PROSE

Many primary texts call for continued investigation, beginning with those of the Anglo-Saxon period, extending into Provençal and Celtic literature (the Welsh *Mabinogion*, for example), and advancing into the writing of the sixteenth century. *Anglo-Saxon Poetry*, selected and translated by R. K. Gordon (London: Dent, 1954), includes poems such as *Helene* and *Judith* that have not yet been subject to feminist criticism as well as works such as *Beowulf* and "The Wife's Lament" that ask for more attention from the perspective of women's studies than they have received. Frederick Goldin's translations of the *Lyrics of the Troubadours and Trouvères* (Garden City, N.Y.: Anchor Press, 1973) deserves close reading, as do *The Middle English Miracles of the Virgin*, edited by Beverly Boyd (San Marino, Cal.: Huntington Library, 1964; Chrétien de Troyes' *Arthurian Romances*, translated by W. W. Comfort (London: Dent, 1914); the Breton *Lays of Marie de France and Other French Legends*, translated by Eugene Mason (London: Dent, 1954); *Juliana of Norwich*, edited by

Franklin Chambers (London: Gollancz, 1955); and many of *The Works of Geoffrey Chaucer* in the most helpful edition of F. N. Robinson (Boston: Houghton-Mifflin, 1957), particularly *Troilus and Criseyde*, *The Legend of Good Wommen*, and the tales of the Franklin, the Clerk, and the Wife of Bath in *The Canterbury Tales*.

J. H. W. Bennett and G. V. Smithers in *Early Middle English Verse and Prose* (Oxford: Clarendon Press, 1966) and William Matthews in *Later Medieval English Prose* (New York: Appleton-Century-Crofts, 1963) present selections of work farther from the mainstream of Middle English writing. The depictions of women are very interesting also in Osbern Bokenham's *Legendys of Hooly Wummen*, edited by Mary S. Serjeantson (London: E.E.T.S., 1960); in the *Ludus Coventriaie*, edited by K. S. Block (London: E.E.T.S., 1960); and in other medieval plays such as those to be found in *Seven Miracle Plays*, edited by A. Franklin (London: Oxford University Press, 1963).

A study of the female/male personifications in John Gower's *Confessio Amantis*, edited by Russell A. Peck (New York: Holt, Rinehart and Winston, 1968), would yield fascinating results, as would Guillaume de Lorris' and Jean de Meun's in *The Romance of the Rose*, translated by Harry W. Robbins and edited by Charles W. Dunn (New York: E.P. Dutton, 1962). Stylistic analyses of *Hali Meidenhad*, edited by F. J. Furnivall (New York: Greenwood Press, 1969), and *The English Text of the Ancrene Riwle*, edited by E. G. Dobson (London: Oxford University Press, 1972), both texts written for women, might well contribute to our knowledge of whether or not there is a "male" or "female" style. *The Paston Letters*, edited by James Gairdner (New York: AMS Press, 1965), with all their cultural complexities, could cast much light on the female lot. Mary R. Mahl and Helene Koon have composed an introductory work of value and point the way to more specialized study of *The Female Spectator: English Women Writers before 1800* (Bloomington, Indiana: Indiana University Press and The Feminist Press, 1977).

PHILOSOPHY AND HISTORY OF IDEAS

The origins of medieval views on womanhood and motherhood are to be found in good part in the Greek philosophers and in the Judeo-Christian thinkers and are reflected in the cosmology and science as well as in the art of the various epochs. Plato's *Timaeus*, translated by Francis M. Cornford (Indianapolis and New York: Bobbs-Merrill, 1959), and

Aristotle's *De Generatione Animalium*, translated by A. L. Peck (London: Loeb Classics, 1943), seem the best texts to begin with. Sarah Pomeroy in *Goddesses, Whores, Wives and Slaves: Women in Antiquity* (New York: Schocken, 1975) surveys in a controversial but always thoughtful manner the attitude of the Greeks and Romans. Mary Daly's *Beyond God the Father* (Boston: Beacon Press, 1973) is a good starting point for exploration of the medieval church's attitude towards the female sex, while *Religion and Sexism: Images of Women in the Jewish and Christian Traditions*, edited by Rosemary Radford Ruether (New York: Simon and Schuster, 1974), is a provocative anthology of essays leading to many new questions and problems in the history of philosophy. S. J. Copleston in *A History of Philosophy*, volumes 1 and 2 (Westminster, Maryland: The Newman Press, 1963), will lead the reader to the relevant writings of the classical philosophers and the scholastics, including Aquinas.

A number of works in diverse fields force a radical reexamination from a different perspective of traditional philosophical approaches. These range from Frederick Engels' *The Origin of the Family, Private Property and the State*, edited by Eleanor Burke Leacock (New York: International Publishers, 1972), to G. Rattray Taylor's *Sex in History* (New York: Harper & Row, 1970), an astounding work that is really an investigation of Western history. Other works of great interest that border either on psychology or on anthropology are those of Phyllis Chesler, *About Men* (New York: Simon and Schuster, 1978); R. E. L. Masters, *Eros and Evil* (Baltimore: Penguin, 1974); and Phillippe Ariès, *Centuries of Childhood* (New York: Knopf, 1962). Vern L. Bullough's masterly essay on "Medieval Medical and Scientific Views of Women," *Viator* 4 (1973): 486–501, should be read by everyone interested in the history of attitudes towards women, as should Bruno Bettelheim's *Symbolic Wounds* (New York: Collier Books, 1971) and Maurice Valency's *In Praise of Love* (New York: Farrar, Strauss and Giroux, 1975) on the growth of the courtly ethic and the idea of romantic love.

WOMEN'S STUDIES, PSYCHOLOGY, LITERARY CRITICISM

Works that attend specifically to the role of women, in the Middle Ages or in other epochs, and seem necessary preliminaries for further study, include those of J. J. Bachofen, *Myth, Religion, and Mother Right* (Princeton, N.J.: Princeton University Press, 1974); Robert Briffault, *The Mothers* (New York: Grosset and Dunlop, 1963); and Elizabeth Gould

Davis, *The First Sex* (New York: Penguin Books, 1973). Adrienne Rich's *Of Woman Born* (New York: W.W. Norton, 1976) is an eloquent exploration of attitudes towards motherhood. Among several excellent anthologies that succeed Eileen Power's pioneering *Medieval Women*, edited by M. Postan (Cambridge: Cambridge University Press, 1975), are those of L. T. Alridge, *The Role of Women in the Middle Ages* (Albany, N.Y.: State University of New York Press, 1975), and Susan Mosher Stuard, *Women in Medieval Society* (University of Pennsylvania Press, 1976).

In psychology, Karen Horney's *Feminine Psychology*, edited by Harold Kelman (New York: W.W. Norton, 1967), and Helene Deutsch's *The Psychology of Women: Motherhood*, vol. 1 (New York: Greene and Stratten, 1944) are basic despite their Freudian limitations. Kate Millett's *Sexual Politics* (Garden City, N.Y.: Doubleday and Co., 1970) remains indispensable as a guide for the reading of male-authored literature, while Erich Neumann's *Amor and Psyche: The Psychic Development of the Feminine* (New York and Evanston: Harper and Row, 1962) manages to arrive at psychological, literary, and feminist readings of great sensitivity in its interpretation of myth.

INDEX

abbesses, 106-114
  in Anglo-Saxon times, 108-9
  in Malory, 107
Abbess-tradition, 108-110
absence, maternal, 4
Adventures at Tarn Wadling, The,
  74-75
anchoresses, 28-31
Anglo-Saxon culture, women in,
  18-19, 93
Anne, Saint, 52-53
antiquity, women in, 7, 63
Aquinas, Saint Thomas, 5
Aristotle, 5
Artemis, 8
Auerbach, Nina, 93

beheading game, 71
Belmont, Mrs. O. H. P., 93
Bennett, H. S., 13n
Beowulf, 18, 93
Beroul
  Tristan and Iseult, 73-74,
  94-98
Bettelheim, Bruno, 4, 86n
Biller, Henry B., 36n
Birgitta, Saint, 118

Bokenham, Osbern, 24
  Legendys of Hooly Wummen,
  24-28, 40-44
*Book of the Knight of the Tour-
  Landry, The,* 46-47
Brangain, 94-98
Briffault, Robert
  The Mothers, 39, 64
Bullough, Vern L., 8, 12n, 20, 50
Byrne, Sister Mary, 109

cannabalism, 83
castration, symbolic, 71
Cecilia, Saint, 23
chansons de geste, 130, 138
Chaucer, Geoffrey
  The Canterbury Tales, 3, 23,
  45-46, 66-67, 76
  The Legend of Good Women,
  105
  Troilus and Criseyde, 134-138
Chesler, Phyllis, 4, 139n
Chester plays, 105-6
childbearing, 23
childbirth, 5, 31-32, 54-55, 111-
  112
childrearing, 49-51

"Clerk's Tale, The," 3, 10
Cohn, Norman, 83
Copleston, Frederick, S. J., 11n
courtly ethos, 76, 94-95, 128,
     134-139
Criseyde, 134-138
Cynewulf
     Juliana, 18-21

Daly, Mary, 12n, 24
Dame Sirith, 44-45
daughters
     as dependents, 15-16, 28-29
     education of, 16-17, 33n, 46,
          57
     as nuns, 32, 42, 57
     in *The Paston Letters,* 49-52
Demiurgos, 5
dependency of women
     economic, 39
     on fathers, 15-16
     on other women, 93-122
     psychological, 16, 28-29
de Pisan, Christine, 8, 85
de Troyes, Chrétien
     Cliges, 98-100, 137
     Erec and Enide, 48-49
     Percival, 4
Deutsch, Helene, 64, 116
Dinesen, Isak, 63
Doctrine of Plenitude, 79
Dorigen, 16
Dworkin, Andrea, 39-41, 50

Economou, George D., 134
Elaine, 131-132
Elyzabeth, Saint, 28
embryology
     ancient, 5
     medieval, 15

Empress of Rome, The, 115-
     117
enchantments, 66-67, 75-78
Engels, Frederick, 33n
Eros and Psyche, 68

fabliaux, 44-45
fairy tale device, 21-22
fantasy
     of power, 63-85
     of rescue, 116
     wish-fulfillment, 66
fathers
     benevolent, 20-22, 28-32
     dominating, 6, 24-28
     omnipotent, 16, 23-24, 120
     submission to, 20-28
     substitute, 50
Felicie, Jacqueline, 65
Female Spectator, The, 127-128
feminine-passive role, 17, 22-23,
     57
fin amors, 94
Floris and Blanchefleur, 100-4
friendship
     male, 132
     among women, 93, 128

Gawain, 68-74, 84-85
generation, male, 5, 15
Giles of Rome, 5, 15
Goldin, Frederick, 76
Gower, John
     Confessio Amantis, 78-79
Gray, Francine du Plessix, 93
Green Knight, The, 72-73
Gripkey, Sister Mary, 117
Griselda, 3, 10
Guenevere, 74-75, 106-8, 128-
     132

hagiography, female, 27-28
Hali Meidenhad, 7, 15, 31-32, 111
Harris, Adelaide Evans, 4
Haskell, Ann S., 5, 50-51, 57
Herolt, Johannes, 116
Hewson, M. Anthony, 11n
Horney, Karen, 12n
"How the Good Wife Taught Her Daughter," 57
Humana, Charles, 6

identification, 12n
    by gender, 8-9, 21, 23-24
    with male, 8, 16, 22
    with mothers, 52
identity, female, 23
imagery, Marian, 7
Iseult, 94-98

Jean de Meun, 79-80
Jerome, Saint, 20
Jesus, 118-121
Julian of Norwich, 118-122
Juliana, Saint, 17-20

Kennedy, C. W., 18

ladies-in-waiting, 53-55, 94-95
Launcelot, 128-132
literature
    decorum in medieval, 43-44
    male-authored, 94
    women in popular medieval, 7, 43
Lives of Women Saints of our Countrie of England, The, 110-114
Loathely Lady, 76-79

love
    of mothers and daughters, 42-43
    romantic, 40, 76-78
    womanly, 116
Lucye, Saint, 42-43
Ludus Coventriae, 52

magical power, 63-85
Malory, Sir Thomas
    Le Morte d'Arthur, 128-132
Mantle of Meekness, 20
Map, Sir Walter
    Courtier's Trifles, 132-134
Marharete, 21-23
Marie de France
    Lay of the Ash Tree, The, 53-56
marriage, 16, 33n
Mary, Saint, 30, 52, 105, 114,118
Masters, R. E. L.
    Eros and Evil, 69, 84
matriarchy, 39, 64
midwives, 64-66
"Miracles of the Virgin," 114
Montague, Ashley, 128
Moore, Marianne, 66
Morgan le Fay, 69-72, 128-130
Mort du Roi Artu, La, 106-8
mother-daughter
    bond, 10, 40, 116, 129
    conflict, 49-51
    conspiracy, 68-74
mother-in-law, 64-73
mothers
    active, 49-51, 94
    foster, 93-122
    natural, 139-157
    passive, 48
mundium, 15-16

Nativity of Mary and Christ, The, 105
Needham, Joseph, 11n
Neumann, Erich, 68
Noah's Flood, 105-6
nurse, as mother, 98
nurture, 9, 52

oedipal anxiety, 64
orphans, 21, 94, 135-138

passivity, maternal, 48-49
Paston Letters, The, 49-51
paterfamilias, 6
patriarchy, 12n, 24-28
patrism, 128
Perrette the midwife, 64-65
Philo, 8
Plato, 5, 121
Pomeroy, Sarah
    Women in Antiquity, 7, 63
Power, Eileen, 44, 50
"The Prioress' Tale," 114

queens
    in mothering role, 100-3
    without power, 5

Rich, Adrienne, 3
Richard of Middleton, 5
rivalry
    between women, 39-40, 55,
        128-134
    mother-daughter, 39, 127
Roman de la rose, 79-84

saints, female, 16, 110
Sexton, Anne, 6
sexual segragation, 7, 42, 94
sisterhood, 93-94
"Son of the King of Erin, The,
    67-68

sovereignty, 76
Stevens, Wallace, 127

Taylor, G. Rattray
    Sex in History, 78
Thrupp, Sylvia, 11n
Tour-Landry, Geoffrey de la,
    46-47
Tristan and Iseult, 94-96
Troilus and Criseyde, 134-37

Valency, Maurice, 6, 12n, 130
Venus, 68
Verdier, Philippe, 44
virginity, 8-9, 20, 23, 31-32, 42-
    43, 57, 110
Virgin Mother, 4, 94, 114-122

wardship, 15-16
warrior ethic, 94-95, 128-139
*Wedding of Sir Gawain and Dame
    Ragnell, The,* 75-78
Wife of Bath, 60, 76
witchcraft, 64-65, 69, 70-75,
    83-84
womb envy, 4-5, 86n
    as audience, 48-49
    as betrayers, 74, 83-85, 128-
        130
    education of, 16-17, 46, 63
    fear of, 74-75, 66
    financial power of, 108
    hatred of, 4-6, 44, 72
    as incomplete males, 5
    medical views of, 65
    as protectors, 10, 47
    in religious orders, 108-9
    sense of inferiority in, 57
Woolf, Virginia, 93

Yeats, W. B., 39

About the author

NIKKI STILLER, an American poet, has taught at Hunter College, Tel-Aviv University of New Orleans. She has contributed articles to *College English*, *Midstream*, *Present Tense*, and other publications.